At Issue

Has Technology Increased Learning?

Other Books in the At Issue Series:

At Issue

Has Technology Increased Learning?

Roman Espejo, Book Editor

GREENHAVEN PRESS
A part of Gale, Cengage Learning

GALE
CENGAGE Learning‑

Detroit • New York • San Francisco • New Haven, Conn • Waterville, Maine • London

GALE
CENGAGE Learning™

Christine Nasso, *Publisher*
Elizabeth Des Chenes, *Managing Editor*

© 2009 Greenhaven Press, a part of Gale, Cengage Learning.

Gale and Greenhaven Press are registered trademarks used herein under license.

For more information, contact:
Greenhaven Press
27500 Drake Rd.
Farmington Hills, MI 48331-3535
Or you can visit our Internet site at gale.cengage.com

Articles in Greenhaven Press anthologies are often edited for length to meet page requirements. In addition, original titles of these works are changed to clearly present the main thesis and to explicitly indicate the author's opinion. Every effort is made to ensure that Greenhaven Press accurately reflects the original intent of the authors. Every effort has been made to trace the owners of copyrighted material.

Cover photograph © Todd Davidson/Illustration Works/Corbis.

LIBRARY OF CONGRESS CATALOGING-IN-PUBLICATION DATA

Has technology increased learning? / Roman Espejo, book editor.
    p. cm. -- (At issue)
Includes bibliographical references and index.
ISBN 978-0-7377-4102-5 (hardcover)
ISBN 978-0-7377-4103-2 (pbk.)
1. Educational technology. 2. Computer-assisted instruction. 3. Learning, Psychology of. 4. Video games--Social aspects. I. Espejo, Roman, 1977-
LB1028.3.H375 2009
371.33'4--dc22
                                                      2008029734

Printed in the United States of America
1 2 3 4 5 6 7 12 11 10 09 08

Contents

Introduction

After much delay, speculation, and buzz, Rockstar Games unleashed *Grand Theft Auto IV (GTA IV)* on April 28, 2008. An instant smash, the action video game sold 3.6 million copies worldwide on the day of its release and grossed over $500 million within its first week. *GTA IV* and its predecessors are Rockstar's flagship video games, which are as popular as they are controversial. Avid gamers and industry critics hail the latest installment of *GTA* as a critical success, while the violent content and graphic nature of the video game series have been criticized by numerous psychologists and targeted in a spate of lawsuits.

Although the gritty urban landscapes, harrowing car chases, and bullet-ridden turf wars of *GTA IV* are a far cry from educational video games like *Quest Atlantis* and *Oregon Trail*, David Hutchison, education professor and author of *Playing to Learn: Video Games in the Classroom*, claims he would use the *GTA* video games in an instructional setting: "The *GTA* activity I chose tasks students with creating their own kid-friendly open-world game that doesn't include all the adult content we normally associate with games in this franchise." Hutchison encourages students to think critically about such violent and exploitative content and suggests that teachers openly "deal with controversial ideas related to video games."

While it is improbable that *GTA IV* will make any school district's curriculum, advocates contend that video games are an overlooked high-tech part of the learning experience. James Paul Gee, literacy expert and author of *What Video Games Have to Teach Us About Learning and Literacy*, argues, "Games are denigrated for being violent, or they're just plain ignored.

They shouldn't be. Young gamers today aren't training to be gun-toting carjackers. They're learning how to learn." He further explains that

> The secret of a video game as a teaching machine isn't its immersive 3-D graphics, but its underlying architecture. Each level dances around the outer limits of the player's abilities, seeking at every point to be hard enough to be just doable. In cognitive science, this is referred to as the regime of competence principle, which results in a feeling of simultaneous pleasure and frustration—a sensation as familiar to gamers as sore thumbs. Cognitive scientist Andy diSessa has argued that the best instruction hovers at the boundary of a student's competence.

For young children, ages three and up, Gee suggests that they start with video games such as *Dr. Seuss's Cat in the Hat*, *Pajama Sam*, and *Spy Fox*, while playing with their parents.

However, other researchers and scientists warn against the early use of even the most educational and E-rated video games for children. A recent study asserts that prolonged exposure to images on flat video screens hinders the development of visual skills that are needed for learning, such as adjusting the eye to focus to and from nearby and distant objects. According to Andrea Thau, spokesperson for the American Optometric Association: "Children need appropriate visual stimulation for sight to develop normally. Parents should limit TV and computer games, especially in children under six whose sight is still developing, though the effects occur in older children too." Additionally, Keith Holland, a British pediatric optometry expert, conducted a study of 12,500 children's vision over the last ten years. From his findings, Holland warns, "The reduction in reading skills, along with the vast increase in time spent playing computer games, is linked." He claims that there are mounting cases of 10-year-olds who prematurely focus as if they have the eyes of a 50-year-old, and that many adolescents are growing up with the underdeveloped eye movements of a toddler, which Holland also correlates with increasing video game playing and television watching.

Furthermore, other researchers and experts caution against video games such as the *GTA* series because of the harmful effects of their graphic violence and exploitation. The findings of two studies published in American Psychological Association's *Journal of Personality and Social Psychology* maintain that—in both controlled settings and real life—violent video games increase aggressive thoughts, actions, and behaviors, and because of their engaging, interactive nature, violence in video games can be more dangerous than the violence in television and movies. Psychologists Craig A. Anderson and Karen E. Dill state, "One study reveals that young men who are habitually aggressive may be especially vulnerable to the aggression-enhancing effects of repeated exposure to violent games. The other study reveals that even a brief exposure to violent video games can temporarily increase aggressive behavior in all types of participants." Also, Anderson insists that violent video games do teach, but that they teach violence:

> Violent video games provide a forum for learning and practicing aggressive solutions to conflict situations. In the short run, playing a violent video game appears to affect aggression by priming aggressive thoughts. Longer-term effects are likely to be longer lasting as well, as the player learns and practices new aggression-related scripts that can become more and more accessible for use when real-life conflict situations arise.

The use of video games as an education tool will continue to be a divisive topic among experts, researchers, and educators. Education professor Rodney Riegle observes, "In a global economy dominated by the video game generation, edutainment will inevitably supercede both education and entertainment. Some people believe that the merger of education and entertainment will diminish education." And as everyday life becomes more wired, the role of technology in education and learning merits deeper research, investigation, and discourse. The viewpoints in *At Issue: Has Technology Increased Learning?* examine the issues, theories, and questions surrounding leading-edge technology in the classroom.

1

Technology Can Increase Learning

Laura Coleman

Laura Coleman is associate editor of State News *magazine, published by the Council of State Governments, a nonpartisan, nonprofit organization that serves the executive, judicial and legislative branches of state governments.*

Cutting-edge technology in the classroom—educational software, computers, access to the Internet—is becoming increasingly valuable to education. Educational software and computers can motivate and challenge students by engaging them in complex analysis and problem solving, which help them develop the technology skills needed to succeed in the twenty-first century workplace. Virtual classes can fill gaps in students' curricula—from Advanced Placement courses to electives—and even connect disadvantaged and rural students to nationally board-certified teachers. Furthermore, such technologies can assist teachers and parents through automatic alerts of student attendance and absences as well as emergencies. It is recommended that policy makers ensure that funding for technology is secured for "wiring" schools for success.

Karen Gill, a physics teacher with 16 years experience, is charged with a difficult task: to teach, challenge and motivate a class of high school students.

To help her in her task, Gill's physics lab provides a unique setting at Henry Clay High School, which has 1,900 students and is located in Lexington, Ky. Her classroom is equipped with innovative technology to help engage students, keep them active in classes, enhance their performance, and allow them to collect very accurate data.

"Henry Clay is a fairly typical school," said Greg Drake, coordinator of Instructional Technology for Fayette County Public Schools. "Karen's class is technology rich, but isn't typical of this school."

On a day this fall, for example, Gill's class used Classroom Performance Systems (CPS) to "vote" on the accuracy of their peers' in-class presentations. These "clickers," as the students call them, act as remote controls similar to the remotes audience members use on the television show, "Who Wants to Be a Millionaire." The students' votes then were projected from their remotes to a television at the front of the classroom.

"The kids are using the clickers in class today," said Gill. "They have analyzed some data and are presenting their information. The class will then ask questions about the data the presenters presented and I'll try not to give away whether or not their presentations are correct—and the class will then offer feedback to fix everything."

Students listen to their peers' presentations and ask questions to correct miscalculations and inaccurate data. Then, the clickers—the class votes on whether to accept or reject the final presentation. The accuracy of their votes makes up a portion of each student's class participation grade for the day. And if the critics in the crowd vote not to accept their classmates' final presentation and calculations, they must have questioned the part they consider incorrect.

How did Henry Clay High afford these smart remotes? It didn't.

"I wrote a grant to get those CPS systems," said Gill. "It took about six hours . . . It wasn't that bad."

"But that's a high demand on teachers, given the other responsibilities they have," Drake interjected.

Using Technology in the Classroom

High-tech clickers aren't the only new technology tool teachers find useful. Software and programs, equipment like laptops and virtual school systems are only a few technologies teachers use to enhance students' classroom experiences.

Many school systems realize how necessary it is to make sure students have access to up-to-date, functional computers and Internet availability.

Software and Programs. Software created specifically for educators can enhance a student's experience in nearly every facet of a learning environment. Software programs are available that can help teachers identify a student's weaknesses in content areas, generate tests and practice problems specific to the areas where they need improvement and automatically alert parents if their children are in danger, among a myriad of other tasks.

Gill uses several Web-based systems for students' assignments. One of those programs is WebHomework, a free service through the University of Texas. It assigns all students the same problems, but uses different numbers for each student to decrease temptation to share answers.

Fayette County Public Schools has also begun a partnership with the UCLA IMMEX (Interactive Multi Media Exercises) Project, sponsored by the National Science Foundation. The Web-based IMMEX software provides students with problem scenarios and requires them to use problem-solving skills that integrate concepts with real-life situations. IMMEX problems provide students the resources to develop, test and refine their hypotheses to arrive at solutions to complex problems. It also has a unique assessment component that allows teachers to evaluate student content knowledge and reasoning skills by using the search path maps the software generates.

"My kids call IMMEX WebHomework on steroids," said Gill. "It's a context-rich problem where they have to make decisions and judge what information is essential to solving the problem. It's not quite as difficult as the real world, but you take a step closer to what the real world is."

Just down the road from Henry Clay High School at the three-year-old Edythe J. Hayes Middle School, 800 middle school students report to their classrooms five days a week. And if they don't, their parents know about it automatically.

Hayes Middle School educators use student attendance software to track and record attendance. The software then allows teachers to generate an attendance report and letters to other staff members and parents by using the attendance data. It also integrates with telephone software to automatically call absent students' parents.

Sherri Jo Heise, the school's principal, said parents appreciate this kind of notification. "They expect us to have it," she said. "If a child is absent, it makes an automatic call home. It helps keep them in check.

"The main thing is keeping that child safe," she said. "It goes beyond the learning. It keeps the child safe, too."

Computers and Hardware. Many school systems realize how necessary it is to make sure students have access to up-to-date, functional computers and Internet availability, which will help equip them with skills they need in the 21st century.

In one unique case, however, an entire state committed itself to this goal. The Maine Learning Technology Initiative, a four-year-old program, has equipped more than 32,000 seventh and eighth graders and 4,000 teachers with Apple notebook computers, wireless networks, training and technical support.

"The project in general is trying to look at how we teach and how kids learn and how technology can be used to enhance that process," said Jeff Mao, coordinator of Educational

Technology for the Maine Department of Education. "The real core of what we're trying to do and where most of our attention goes is teacher training and to produce best practices.

"It gets a lot of attention, the fact that we've spent so much money on all this equipment," he said. "But that's not the reason we did this, not to teach kids computer skills. The kids will gain computer skills simply by playing with a computer. We tried to figure out how as an English teacher, you can reach your goals, not if every kid knows how to make a PowerPoint."

Former Maine Gov. Angus King took initial steps toward the project in 1999. "Governor King is very charismatic," said Mao. "He deeply cares about the state, and when he latched on to the idea, he was able to move a crowd and bring people along."

According to Mao, the initiative was born through the governor's desire to move Maine ahead of other states in terms of economic development. "He realized in talking to other governors that if we did the same things other states were doing, we'd stay where we were ranked," said Mao. "To make a change, we must think beyond the simple things."

Mao said King then spoke with professional location specialists—people who advise companies where to open—and asked them what motivated companies to locate to certain areas.

"The number one thing was the able and ready work force," said Mao. "You can always deal with taxes, there are plenty of locations that are near enough to transportation so you can get supplies, but if you don't have an educated work force, you end up spending an enormous amount of money to bring one in or educate one. If the work force already exists somewhere, you can plop the factory down there and let them go."

While it was King who initiated the project, he could not have taken it on alone. "I think what it takes in the end is significant political will at the legislative level. Schools alone can't do what we're doing—there's just not enough money in the traditional school formula," said Mao.

And Maine's legislature made sure school districts didn't have to go it alone. "In the end, if you strip everything away, someone has to pay for this. This is state funded," said Mao. "The legislature supported the project, listened to constituents, decided it was a good program and when it came time to put their thumbs up or down, they put their thumbs up."

To Mao, this initiative helps level the educational playing field. "I think one of the things to look at or consider is that we often talk in state government about equity and serving the population," he said. "When we look at how schools are funded, we say it's equitable, but it's a separate but equal kind of equitable. In a school district, the funding formula gives fewer dollars per head to richer districts than to those which are economically depressed. This makes sense.

"But on the other hand, we look at how our project was deployed, and it was a different kind of equity," he said. "Every student and every teacher was given the device and training. It gets all the way down to the classroom level."

Virtual Schools. Where laptops grant access to computer equipment to students who may not have it at home, virtual schools can help increase accessibility to classes and teachers some students would not normally be able to experience.

"The number one advantage to virtual schools is that they provide courses irrespective of where students reside," said Bill Thomas, director of the Southern Regional Education Board. "They can be used to fill gaps in curricula, whether it is with Advanced Placement courses, core subjects or things people refer to as electives."

Thomas said 12 of the 16 SREB states already provide Web-based courses, with Florida leading the pack. Florida's program began in 1997, and this year alone, more than 40,000 high school student are taking online courses. The program is funded by the state.

"Schools only get money from the state if a student has successfully completed the course," said Thomas, noting that Florida requires that students pass the class.

Success rates in Florida range from 90 to 92 percent. Of the 137 students who took Advanced Placement courses through Florida's virtual school in 2000–2001, more than half earned scores of 4 or 5—on a five-point scale—on the exams. About 65 percent of the students earned scores of 3 or higher—besting the national average of 61 percent.

If education is a top priority, policymakers have to provide for better technology in the classroom.

"We see these programs as good economics," said Thomas. "Why should everybody create all courses? Once online courses are developed, teachers can teach the same course and make copies of it. You could have five or 50 algebra teachers teaching that course."

The best part of virtual schools, said Thomas, is that the programs are closely monitored no matter where the students are. "Rural kids or inner city kids who have never had access to a quality teacher can have a nationally board certified teacher," he said.

"Just Do It"

To Reg Weaver, president of the National Education Association, it's as simple as this: If education is a top priority, policymakers have to provide for better technology in the classroom.

"When America decides something is important, they find the money," said Weaver. "I'd say to policymakers, when it comes to making America strong, when it comes to making sure America has the people to make sure we are the country we are today, to have a quality public education, they need to be like Nike and just do it to make sure schools have the money they need."

2

Technology May Not Increase Learning

Patrick Welsh

Patrick Welsh has been an English teacher at T.C. Williams High School in Alexandria, Virginia, for over thirty years.

The obsession of some school administrators with obtaining the most innovative and cutting-edge technology for their schools is leaving teachers and students in the dark. Not all teachers find it more effective—or even easier—to teach with laptops, hand-held devices, and other high-tech gizmos, which have begun to force out traditional, proven methods of teaching. Also, many teachers are being turned off by having to adjust and learn how to use new, extraneous devices and software. Laptops in the classroom frequently disconnect from wireless servers and applications crash, wasting class time. The rush to adopt the latest educational technology may impress school administrators and principals, but it is not a quick fix to academic performance gaps or a shortcut to learning.

What's wrong with the teachers at T.C. Williams High School?

[In] September [2007], we moved into a new $98 million building in Alexandria, [Virginia] one of the most expensive high schools ever built. Natural light floods the classrooms, and each one is equipped with a ceiling-mounted LCD projector, which transfers anything I can put on my laptop computer—from poetry readings at the Library of Congress to YouTube interviews with Toni Morrison and other writers—onto a large screen at the front of the room. Students' behavior seems much improved: A cafeteria that looks like something out of an upscale mall has had a curiously pacifying effect on them, as has the presence of 126 security cameras.

So you'd think T.C. teachers would be ecstatic. But it's just the opposite—faculty morale is the lowest and cynicism the highest I've seen in years. The problem? What a former Alexandria school superintendent calls "technolust"—a disorder affecting publicity-obsessed school administrators nationwide that manifests itself in an insatiable need to acquire the latest, fastest, most exotic computer gadgets, whether teachers and students need them or want them. Technolust is in its advanced stages at T.C., where our administrators have made such a fetish of technology that some of my colleagues are referring to us as "Gizmo High."

"Paperless" Classrooms

Science and math teachers, for instance, have been told that they can't use traditional overhead projectors to present material to classes, even though the teachers say that in many cases, they're far superior to computers for getting certain concepts across. But the measure of teachers now is not whether they can convey their subject matter to students but how "paperless" their classrooms are—how many new gizmos they use. To paraphrase the movie *Field of Dreams*, if a computer company makes a classroom gizmo, the Alexandria school system will buy it.

The latest is the "school pad"—a hand-held device that allows a teacher to roam around the room and underline whatever the LCD projects onto the screen. In other words, it saves teachers from walking a few feet to their desks to click the computer mouse. The school system ordered 77 school pads for T.C. at $495 apiece, even though one teacher said they reminded her of "the Magna Doodle pads we had as kids. It's another way to waste money for people who are too lazy to write on the board."

For a while, I thought it was just older teachers like me—immigrants to the Internet world—who were chafing at the so-called technology initiative, but it turns out that even the youngest teachers are fed up. "They would rather have a cyborg teaching than me," one young English teacher complained to me. "It's technology for the sake of technology—not what works or helps kids learn, but what makes administrators look good, what the public will think is cutting edge."

Too many school systems are becoming device-driven— they're buying computer devices because they're there.

The school admits as much on its Web site, which includes this entry addressing teachers:

"Imagine this headline: '[Alexandria City Public Schools] Recognized for its Premiere Educational Technology Program, Student Achievement Correlated to Technology Implementation.' What kind of technology exists at the high school that would create a headline like this?"

Principals and other administrators may live off headlines, but teachers live off whether their students learn. "Teachers shouldn't have to change how they teach to fit some technological device," said Peter Cevenini, who heads up the K-12 education division of Cisco's Internet Business Solutions Group. "Teaching is a craft, and many great teachers instruct in totally different ways. Too many school systems are becoming device-driven—they're buying computer devices because they're there."

Kids certainly aren't fooled by all the gizmos. "The most effective teacher I have is Mr. Nickley," said senior Jamal Stone. "He isn't into all this computer stuff. All he uses is the board—

the whole board. He's lively, energetic, witty and really knows his math. He forces you to pay attention; you can't drift off even if you want to."

Stone said he feels sorry for many of the "paperless" teachers who are always having students use their school-issued laptops in class. "The teachers think their students are engrossed in class research when they're actually playing video games and surfing the Net," he said. "Whenever the computer Nazis block one game, kids just find new ones." Senior Katerina Savchyn confirmed that she sometimes uses her laptop to escape the boredom of class by playing the online "Helicopter Game."

In fact, the school-issued laptops are a problem in many ways. Students say all kinds of class time is wasted as they struggle to upload programs for class. The laptops constantly fail to connect to the wireless server, even though the computer geeks came around to every classroom a few months ago and installed new memory in every computer. The school system, which rushed into giving kids laptops [in 2005], is constantly trying to play catch up with the technology.

Technology Overkill

What's truly disconcerting is that the technology overkill is turning off talented young teachers. As one of the best here—someone whom parents seek out and students love—put it: "There's a lot of things I like about the computers, but we're being forced to do an unreasonable number of computer activities. Many of them don't fit my teaching style. We have so many hoops to jump through that some days I come in and I'm not excited to teach. All the computer activities just take us away from students."

The administration doesn't seem to care about that. Recently, we English teachers had to get substitutes for our classes and attend an all-day technology session. An e-mail from the central office informed us that we would "examine methods for integrating technology to deepen student understanding by increasing rigor, creating relevance and building relationships with students and among students."

Apparently administrators really do believe that computers are the key to building relationships. The human voice and face-to-face contact have been replaced by e-mail and Blackboard, a computer program that allows teachers and students to communicate via the Internet. I've always thought that in some ways schools should be like families, but as one experienced teacher puts it, "We're becoming like a correspondence school where all communication is faceless."

You can walk around T.C. and peer into offices and classrooms and see administrators, guidance counselors and teachers staring at their computers instead of interacting with students. To some, T.C.'s principal of two years seems more comfortable in cyberspace than in face-to-face interaction. His preferred method of communicating with teachers seems to be via e-mail, and some say they think he doesn't know who they are or what they teach.

I love my computer and all I can do with it; on the few days when it's been in for repairs, I've felt a bit lost at first, the way I do when I can't find my cellphone or my TiVo remote. But as classes go on, I feel much closer to my students without the distraction of the laptop.

[Technology] will never replace good teaching.

Just a Tool

Of course, the big question isn't whether teachers like spending their time learning one new gizmo after another, but whether a parade of new technologies will help kids learn. From what I can see, that's not the case. Says one math teacher: "Math grows out of the end of a pencil. You don't want the quick answer; you want students to be able to develop the answer, to discover the why of it. The administration seems to think that computers will make math easy, but it has to be a painful, step-by-step process."

A social studies teacher agrees. More than ever, he says, "our students want to push a button or click a mouse for a quick A, B or C answer. Fewer and fewer of them want to think anymore because good thinking takes time."

I see the same thing in my classes, especially when it comes to writing essays. Many students send their papers in over the Internet, and while the margins are correct and the fonts attractive, the writing is worse than ever. It's as if the rule is: Write one draft, run spell check, hit "send" and pray.

Alexandria isn't the only school system bitten by the technology bug. Many rushed into giving every student a laptop in the hopes of finding a quick fix to the technological and academic performance gaps between the well-to-do and those less so. But now, a number are abandoning the programs, saying there's no evidence that the laptops are helping students academically—and that they may even be a distraction.

North Point High School for Science, Technology and Industry in Waldorf went with ceiling-mounted LCD projectors but nixed the idea of laptops for all students. "Our philosophy is to have whatever technology our teachers want to do their jobs better available to them," Principal Kim Hill told me. "Technology is just a tool, not an end in itself. It will never replace good teaching."

Are you listening, Alexandria?

3

Technology Can Increase Learning for Students with Learning Disabilities

DO-IT/University of Washington

DO-IT (Disabilities, Opportunities, Internetworking and Technology) is a project based at the University of Washington, Seattle, that helps individuals with disabilities transition to college and careers.

Everyday technology and software, along with specialized devices and applications, can help students with learning and other disabilities reach their learning potential and higher levels of academic achievement. Such students may face challenges with spoken or written language, or with arithmetic and reasoning, and the appropriate technology or software can help them compensate for their disabilities. For instance, simple word processors can assist students who suffer from dyslexia with spelling- and grammar-checking applications, and modified products such as speech recognition software and talking calculators can be useful to students with a variety of disabilities. Even "simple" technologies such as Post-It Notes and highlighter pens can offer ingeniously simple solutions in organizing thoughts, ideas, and concepts.

A specific learning disability (LD) is in most situations a "hidden disability." Because there are no outward signs of a disability such as a white cane or wheelchair, people with an

LD are often neglected when considering adaptive computer technology. However, many people with learning disabilities can benefit from mainstream and specialized hardware and software to operate a computer and further their academic and career goals.

Definitions and Terminology

A specific learning disability is unique to the individual and can appear in a variety of ways. It may be difficult to diagnose, to determine impact, and to accommodate.

Generally speaking, someone may be diagnosed with a learning disability if he/she is of average or above-average intelligence and there is a lack of achievement at age and ability level, or a large discrepancy between achievement and intellectual ability.

Assistive and adaptive technology does not "cure" a specific learning disability. These tools compensate rather than remedy, allowing a person with [a learning disability to] demonstrate his intelligence and knowledge.

An untrained observer may conclude that a person with a learning disability is "lazy" or "just not trying hard enough." He may have a difficult time understanding the large discrepancy between reading comprehension and proficiency in verbal ability. The observer sees only the input and output, not the processing of the information. Deficiencies in the processing of information make learning and expressing ideas difficult or impossible tasks. Learning disabilities usually fall within four broad categories:

- *Spoken language*—listening and speaking.

- *Written language*—reading, writing and spelling.

- *Arithmetic*—calculation and concepts.

- *Reasoning*—organization and integration of ideas and thoughts.

A person with a learning disability may have discrepancies in one or all of these categories. The effects of an LD are manifested differently for different individuals and range from mild to severe. Learning disabilities may also be present along with other disabilities such as mobility or sensory impairments. Often people with Attention Deficit Disorder/Attention Deficit Hyperactive Disorder (ADD/ADHD) also have learning disabilities. Specific types of learning disabilities include:

1. *Dysgraphia*—An individual with Dysgraphia has a difficult time with the physical task of forming letters and words using a pen and paper and has difficulty producing legible handwriting.

2. *Dyscalculia*—A person with Dyscalculia has difficulty understanding and using math concepts and symbols.

3. *Dyspraxia*—Language comprehension of a person with Dyspraxia does not match language production. She may mix up words and sentences while talking.

4. *Non-verbal Learning Disorder*—A Non-verbal Learning Disorder is demonstrated by below-average motor coordination, visual-spatial organization, and social skills.

5. *Dyslexia*—An individual with Dyslexia may mix up letters within words and words within sentences while reading. He may also have difficulty spelling words correctly while writing; letter reversals are common. Some individuals with Dyslexia may also have a difficult time with navigating and route finding using right/left and/or compass directions.

Accommodations

Assistive and adaptive technology does not "cure" a specific learning disability. These tools compensate rather than remedy, allowing a person with an LD [to] demonstrate his intelligence and knowledge. Adaptive technology for the person with an LD is a made-to-fit implementation. Trial and error may be required to find a set of appropriate tools and techniques for a specific individual. Ideally, a person with an LD plays a key role in selecting her technology. She should help to determine what works and what does not. Once basic tools and strategies are selected, they can be "test driven," discarded, adapted, and/or refined.

Following are descriptions of some computing tools that have been used effectively by individuals with specific learning disabilities. This list is not exhaustive and should not limit the person with an LD or the adaptive technology practitioner from trying something new. Today's experimental tinkering could lead to tomorrow's commonly used tool.

Word Processors Computer-based accommodations for Dyslexia may not require specialized hardware or software. For example, a person with Dyslexia can benefit from regularly using built-in word processor features such as:

- Spell checking.

- Grammar checking.

- Font size and color changes.

These built-in features are relatively low priced tools that, when used together, provide an alternative to handwritten expression. The use of spell checkers can allow the person with learning difficulties to remain focused on the task of communication rather than getting bogged down in the process of trying unsuccessfully to identify and correct spelling errors. Many word processing programs also include tools for outlining thoughts and providing alternative visual formats that may compensate for difficulty in organizing words and ideas. Additionally, color-coded text options and outline capabilities present in many word processing programs are useful tools for those with difficulty sorting and sequencing thoughts and ideas. Additionally, color-coded text options and outline capabilities present in many word processing programs are useful tools for those with difficulty sorting and sequencing thoughts and ideas.

Some individuals have difficulty organizing and integrating thoughts and ideas while writing. Concept mapping software allows for visual representation of ideas and concepts.

A word processor can also be used as a compensatory tool for a person with Dysgraphia. Use of a keyboard may be a viable alternative for an individual who has difficulty expressing his thoughts via handwriting.

Reading Systems. An individual who can take in information through listening much better than by reading may benefit from using a reading system. These systems allow text on screen (document, web page or email) to be read aloud through the computer's sound card. A scanner and Optical Character Recognition (OCR) software (e.g., Freedom Scientific's WYNN or Kurzweil 3000) adds the feature of reading printed text. Hard copy text is placed on the scanner where it is converted into a digital image. This image is then converted to a text file, making the characters recognizable by the computer. The computer can then read the words back using a speech synthesizer and simultaneously present the words on screen.

Reading systems include options such as highlighting a word, sentence, or paragraph using contrasting colors. If desired, the reader may elect to have only one word at a time appear on the screen to improve her grasp of the material. Increasing the size of the text displayed on the screen as well as changing text color can increase reading comprehension for some people with specific learning disabilities.

Concept Mapping. Some individuals have difficulty organizing and integrating thoughts and ideas while writing. Concept mapping software allows for visual representation of ideas and concepts. These representations are presented in a physical manner and can be connected with arrows to show the relationship between ideas. These graphically represented ideas can be linked, rearranged, color coded, and matched with a variety of icons to suit the need of the user. Concept mapping software can be used as a structure for starting and organizing such diverse writing projects as poetry, term papers, resumes, schedules, or even computer programs.

Phonetic Spelling. People with Dyslexia often spell phonetically, making use of word prediction or spell checking software less useful. Devices (e.g., Franklin Electronic Dictionary™) or software (YakYak™) that renders phonetic spelling into correctly spelled words may be useful tools.

Word Prediction. Spelling words correctly while typing can be a challenge for some people with Dyslexia. Word prediction programs prompt the user with a list of most likely word choices based upon what has been typed so far. Rather than experiencing the frustration of remembering the spelling of a word, he can refer to the predictive list, choose the desired word and continue with the expression of thoughts and ideas.

Speech Recognition. Speech recognition products provide appropriate tools for individuals with a wide range of learning disabilities. Speech recognition software takes the spoken word via a microphone and converts it to machine-readable format. The user speaks into a microphone either with pauses between words (discrete speech) or in a normal talking manner (continuous speech). The discrete product, although slower, is often the better choice for those with LDs because identifying errors can be done as they occur. Making corrections after the fact using continuous speech requires good reading skills.

Speech recognition technology requires that the user have moderately good reading comprehension to correct the program's text output. Because many people with LDs have reading problems, speech recognition is not always an appropriate accommodation.

Organizational Software/Personal Information Managers (PIMs). Organizing schedules and information is difficult for some people with Dyslexia and/or Non-verbal Learning Disorder. Personal Information Managers (PIMs) such as a Palm Pilot™ or Casio™ or organizational software such as Microsoft Outlook™ or Lotus Organizer™ can accommodate these disabilities. Such tools can be helpful to those with LDs by providing a centralized and portable means of organizing schedules and information. The cues provided by these tools can assist keeping on task and may help provide visual alternatives to represent what work needs to be done and what has been accomplished. However, they may also put early learners at a disadvantage by requiring yet another program and interface to learn and remember to use. Individuals may lack the discipline/attention skills to regularly check the application/device.

Talking Calculators. A talking calculator is an appropriate tool for people with Dyscalculia. The synthesized voice output of a talking calculator provides feedback to the user that helps them identify any input errors. Additionally, hearing the calculated answer can provide a check against the transposition of numbers commonly reversed in reading by people with Dyslexia or Dyscalculia.

Low Tech Tools (Post-It Notes, Highlighters). Not all assistive technology for people with LDs is computer-based. The use of common office supplies such as Post-It Notes™ and highlighter pens provide elegantly simple means of sorting and prioritizing thoughts, ideas, and concepts. Often, tools of one's

own making provide the most effective and comfortable accommodations for learning difficulties.

4

Some Schools Are Left Behind in Educational Technologies

Dave Zielinski

Dave Zielinski is a contributor to Presentations *magazine, a periodical dedicated to business management.*

Expected to be renewed in 2008, the No Child Left Behind Act (NCLB) was signed by president George W. Bush in 2002, aiming to set state and national standards in the classroom partly through educational technology. However, these ambitious goals are challenging to meet: Not all schools receive adequate or equal funding for these technologies, which include laptops, electronic whiteboards, and software. The NCLB may not adequately inform school administrators of how much funds their schools are entitled to and how they can be acquired. And even though technology literacy can improve student performance, it is left stalling, as such funding is not prioritized as highly as boosting math and reading scores. Through the NCLB, the money for technologically upgrading schools is available, but it is up to school administrators to make sure their schools are receiving it.

Ask Sheryl McNellis about the U.S. federal government's No Child Left Behind Act (NCLB) and you'll likely hear raves about the controversial law being a lifeline for her school district's technology budget, allowing the purchase of new presentation technologies and investments in teacher training that otherwise wouldn't have been possible. As technology co-

Dave Zielinski, "No Nickel Left Behind," *Presentations*, vol. 18, September 2004, pp. 31–35. Copyright © 2004 VNU Business Media. Article used with permission of Nielsen Business Media, Inc.

ordinator of Wagon Mound Public Schools in Wagon Mound, N.M., McNellis tapped NCLB funds for buying personal digital assistants (PDAs) to aid teachers in boosting K-3 student reading skills, interactive whiteboards to create more individualized instruction for special education classes, and videoconferencing equipment to help educate teachers statewide on the district's best practices for improving student reading achievement.

Many school administrators are unsure about how much technology-related funding is still available.

You'll hear similar kudos for the landmark law from Sharon Smith, director of special projects for the Apache Junction Unified School District in Apache Junction, Ariz. Smith used $108,000 in federal NCLB funds in the 2003–2004 school year for laptop computers, electronic response systems, document cameras, projectors and electronic whiteboards, and for training teachers to use this technology within their curriculums.

But plenty of other public school administrators, teachers, legislators—and presentation technology vendors—have a less generous view of the relatively new law, which is the most significant federal education legislation in a generation. Many feel the No Child Left Behind Act sets ambitious new goals and timelines for student achievement—including targets for use of new learning technologies in the classroom and enhancing the technical literacy of students—but doesn't sufficiently fund those performance mandates. More voices continue to join that resistance. [In the summer of 2004], for example, Wisconsin Attorney General Peg Lautenschlager issued an opinion holding that the state has no legal obligation to implement the NCLB because it fails to adequately fund student testing and other activities the act requires. And according to a report from the National Conference of State

Legislatures, as many as 20 states have explored ways to end their participation in No Child Left Behind, asking for more funding to implement the law, or looking for ways to change the law itself.

While some of this dissent can be chalked up to partisan political squabbling, for many school administrators—and the technology manufacturers who sell education products—it's more a matter of uncertainty and rancor about the law's funding formulas than any sort of political maneuvering. Many school administrators are unsure about how much technology-related funding is still available, how much of that money they might qualify for, and how to go about applying for the funds. Many believe, rightly or wrongly, that federal and state educational bodies have done a less-than-stellar job of publicizing how much NCLB funding is available for instructional technology buys, which technologies are eligible for federal funding, and what the criteria are for awarding competitive-grant funds.

The good news is that in most states, there is more money available for technology purchases than most educators realize—and it's waiting there for those who can figure out how to get it. The U.S. government has allocated more than $700 million for implementation of the No Child Left Behind Act, much of it specifically earmarked for educational technology and technology training. The key to getting a piece of that pie—thereby ensuring that schools don't miss valuable opportunities to supplement their technology budgets, and vendors don't miss opportunities to serve their public-education clients—lies in thoroughly understanding the goals, processes and hurdles of the NCLB Act itself.

Whither NCLB Tech Funding?

Signed into law in 2002, the No Child Left Behind Act affects almost every public school in America. Focused on improving the performance of disadvantaged students, the law holds states and schools more accountable for student progress by requiring annual testing of third- through eighth-graders in reading and math. It also requires schools to bring all students up to the "proficient" level on state tests by the 2013–2014 school year. And the law asks schools receiving federal Title I funds (schools in which at least 40 percent of the students are from low-income families) to meet "adequate yearly progress" benchmarks toward performance goals or face the possibility of sanctions.

All of those different programs, which on the surface don't look like education technology opportunities, can be used to help fund technology services and hardware or software.

The law's key program for technology funding is called Enhancing Education Through Technology, or Title II Part D. It's designed to help schools meet the NCLB Act's goals of improving academic achievement through technology and blending that technology into teacher training and curriculum development. According to the U.S. Department of Education. $700 million in federal formula-based grants has been made available through Title II Part D.

What isn't well-known in the education and vendor communities is that many of the NCLB law's other titles and programs provide technology-related funding as well. NCLB programs such as Title I, Reading First, teacher-quality, and migrant-education funds all have dollars available for technology spending, as long as the technology is used to further the primary goal of the those specific programs.

"All of those different programs, which on the surface don't look like education technology opportunities, can be used to help fund technology services and hardware or software," said John Bailey, director of educational technology for the U.S. Department of Education, during a recent teleconference on the NCLB Act.

For example, the Apache Junction school district taps Title I funds to pay for teaching specialists who oversee technology-based learning programs for students at risk of falling short of the standards. These funds are designed to help supplement, not replace, a district's operational budget. In other words, says the district's Sharon Smith, "I can't take Title I funds and go pay for a new third-grade teacher, but I can use them for afterschool programs involving learning technologies."

Districts that don't believe in the power of technology to aid learning and achievement usually choose to buy more textbooks and raise teacher salaries.

While some of the criticism about insufficient funding for the No Child Left Behind Act is grounded in the shrinking amount of Title I allocations to certain states and districts (amounts based on the latest census data of students living in poverty), it's also clear that some school administrators haven't taken full advantage of the technology funding options available to them through the law.

"Some school districts are very aggressive in seeking NCLB funds through the law's competitive-grant process, and others are not," says Bob Troidl, a former school principal and technology director who's now an account executive with PolyVision Corp. in Phoenix. "My belief is schools find money for what they really want to find money for. Some schools really believe in technology and work hard to find the funds to pay for it." Troidl adds that districts that don't believe in the power of technology to aid learning and achievement usually choose to buy more textbooks and raise teacher salaries, rather than consider technology improvements in the classroom. "Part of the reason for that is we still don't have enough good research to show how technology can pay off in improved student achievement," he says.

And although U.S. Education Department officials talk up the importance of technology in supporting key NCLB objectives, technology issues clearly don't carry the same weight as other goals in the law for reading and math improvement or upgrading teaching quality. NCLB objectives for enhancing students' technology literacy, for example, lack the bite of many of the law's other mandates.

Competitive-grant Funds Play Key Role

One district that's made effective use of competitive-grant funds received through the law's Enhancing Education Through Technology program is the previously mentioned Wagon Mound Public School District in New Mexico. In the 2003–2004 school year the district supplemented $3,700 in state formula-based funding with $111,000 in competitive-grant monies used for new learning technologies and associated teacher training.

Wagon Mound received a three-year Reading First grant that paid for 25 PDAs that teachers use to assess and improve the reading skills of kindergarten through third-grade students. NCLB funds also enabled the school district to purchase projectors, computers, digital cameras, printers and scanners for various learning purposes. In addition, Wagon Mound received another $50,000 through the NCLB's Individuals with Disabilities Education Act (IDEA) to buy whiteboard-capture products (which turn standard whiteboards into digital tools) as well as adaptive technologies and amplifiers that help enhance the learning experience for students who are deaf, near-deaf or autistic.

The Wagon Mound School District also used NCLB monies to hire a half-time technology coach to advise district teachers on the most effective ways to integrate new hardware and software into the district's curriculum. "The last thing we wanted to do is spend a lot of money on technology toys, then leave teachers to fend for themselves on the best ways to use the technology to improve student achievement," says Sheryl McNellis, the district's technology coordinator.

How was the school district made aware of these multiple grant opportunities? The New Mexico state education department advertises NCLB competitive-grant competitions on its Web site and regularly sends e-mail and other correspondence to its school districts explaining conditions and timelines for upcoming grant competitions. But it also pays for school administrators and technology coordinators to be proactive and ready to write these grants, says McNellis: "You have to know when these grants are opening up and have a good plan for pursuing them."

New Mexico, as well as many other states, holds regional conferences that offer instruction on writing effective grants, and provide information on where to find the best "scientifically proven, research-based" teaching methods the No Child Left Behind Act uses as criteria for making certain funding decisions. In addition, New Mexico holds workshops for technology vendors to help them tailor product-marketing approaches in ways that dovetail with NCLB technology goals and funding formulas.

Strong Leadership Drives Funding Success

A recent study of more than 450 K-12 school districts, cosponsored by The Consortium for School Networking (CoSN) and the research firm Grunwald Associates, found that stagnant or shrinking technology budgets threaten funding for six out of every 10 school districts. But the study also found that with "visionary leadership and strong community support," many school districts were able to bolster their technology plans and budgets. Those schools committed to deepening the impact of technology in education find ways to raise or repurpose funds to maintain or increase their level of support for technology, even in difficult budgeting cycles, says Keith Krueger, CEO of CoSN.

Apache Junction Unified School District in Arizona is among the districts that have worked hard to build both school board and community support for use of technology as a way to improve achievement and prepare students to function in a technology-dependent society. The nine-school, 6,000-student district used $85,000 in NCLB Title II D funds to equip five classrooms with new hardware and software designed to create more individualized learning and help teachers assess student skill levels—and craft plans for improvement—with more speed and accuracy.

The district has also pooled NCLB dollars with funds received through other resources, such as the Carl Perkins Vocational and Technical Education Act, to purchase document cameras, portable projectors, electronic and dry-erase whiteboards, tablet PCs and audience response systems (used to assess content retention and diagnose student learning needs). The Apache Junction High School also has a full complement of the latest application and design software for student use in commercial art, photography, music and other classes.

Of total NCLB funds the district received in 2003–2004, 11 percent (or $108,000) was spent on technology-related purchases, says Sharon Smith, the district's director of special projects. "Technology resources available through the No Child Left Behind Act have helped us to become more technology-savvy in how we assess and track student progress and support learning objectives. No Child also gives us more flexibility in how we can spend federal funds than previous legislation did."

Given its scope and impact, the No Child Left Behind Act is sure to inspire more controversy and debate in the years ahead. But despite its perceived limitations, there's little debating that the law does in fact help public school districts throughout the country enrich learning by acquiring instructional technologies and funding teacher training, so it behooves all eligible schools and districts to make sure they're getting their fair share of the pie.

5

Computers in Classrooms Can Increase Learning

Rich Davis

Rich Davis is a staff writer for the Evansville Courier and Press *in Evansville, Indiana.*

Just as the technologies before it are on their way out, computers in the classroom are becoming commonplace, to the benefit of teachers, parents, and students. They allow teachers to use electronic grade books, which parents can have access to and track their children's grades and academic progress. Computers and the Internet put information at teachers' fingertips, allowing them to teach in the moment rather than adhere to a prepared lesson. The technologies and software that come with computers, such as podcasting and on-demand streaming videos, engage students. Classrooms still seem the same as they did twenty years ago, but the expanding ways computers can be used in teaching and learning are changing that.

It's said that, in the 1830s, a well-educated teacher from out East came to the Evansville [Indiana] area and introduced a blackboard into his classroom.

Apparently, some people thought it was a lazy way to teach, for when he opened the school's clapboard door one morning, a critic had scrawled on the board:

"Any man of common sense, would throw the blackboard over the fence."

At the end of the term, the teacher and the blackboard had to go.

Jason Bailey finds the anecdote amusing, but then, he would.

He's one of six "integrating curriculum and technology specialists" (iCats) with the Evansville-Vanderburgh School Corp. [EVSC], all former classroom teachers now helping fellow educators get over the learning curve of new technology.

One recent morning inside the lab at the Christa McAuliffe Professional Development Center north of Downtown, Bailey watched as Candice Dodson gave Bosse High School world history teacher Bob Rogers pointers on using the electronic grade book.

"I'm not the first one to jump when something new comes along," chuckles Rogers, an 81-year-old who started teaching in Peru, Kan., in 1949 and recalls the EVSC's first computer, "Downtown—in the 1970s—took up half a basement," he says.

[Classroom] computers have made learning so much more real-time.

In 20 minutes Rogers felt fairly comfortable with the electronic grade book, an online system into which teachers input data that are accessible to parents.

Parents can log on with a password and monitor their child's grades, schedule, standardized tests and assignments, and even see if they've been tardy or had a discipline problem.

And it helps kids, too, says Dodson, a former elementary teacher.

"They can self-monitor, see where they missed an assignment or should have studied harder for a quiz."

Dodson and Bailey say the casual observer visiting a classroom today wouldn't notice many changes from 20 years ago, although VCRs are obsolete, not to mention 16mm projectors.

We're still a few years away from every student having a computer screen built into his desk, but many schools have computer labs or mobile laptop carts that can be wheeled in.

"When I started (teaching) 13 years ago, if you had a computer in your classroom, it meant you'd written a grant for it," says Bailey, who formerly taught English at Harrison High School.

Par for the Course

Today, a computer for the teacher is par for the course.

What's changing, the two trainers explain, are the expanded ways a classroom computer can be used.

Among devices finding their way into classrooms are document cameras plugged into the computer and a digital projector often hanging from the ceiling. It creates a "presentation station."

A teacher can plop down a picture or page out of a book and immediately show her class what she's talking about.

Better yet, beyond playing DVDs, some teachers can now access United Streaming—video-on-demand—and play video "segments" through the computer or projector.

"The beauty is it breaks down videos by chapter," says Dodson. "If I was teaching about Saturn, for example, I could just take the part on Saturn (not the entire 30-minute video on the solar system)."

She says the use of technology varies.

"Kindergartners still need to write their letters and go find A on the floor but for teachers, the computer is a valuable piece of equipment that makes our lives easier.

"I remember when I was studying to become a teacher (more than 20 years ago). They'd tell us to design a lesson. You'd have to think it up, write it out, go cut and paste, find pictures in magazines. If you wanted something on Eskimos, you better find pictures of Eskimos. Today, you might go to a fifth-grade lesson plan site, type in 'Eskimo' and 'fifth-grade lesson,' and a huge amount of resources comes up.

"If I'm a teacher and one of my students says, 'What is the Iditarod?,' I can go in and find a picture immediately, show the kids the dogs, the route. I don't have to say, 'Well, tomorrow we'll talk about it.' Computers have made learning so much more real-time . . . you don't lose that teaching moment when everyone is tuned in."

She also works with teachers on how to do podcasts. One fifth-grade teacher, she said, "noticed her students got more excited about their book reports" when an audio podcast showed the book cover and carried the voice of the student reading his report.

While Rogers uses a computer and sees its merits, especially for research by older students, he holds to some old ways and doesn't hide his disdain for standardized tests.

"Kids are no different today than when I started, just better informed. . . . The trouble with education today is that we have forgotten that we are not all the same."

He will continue to keep paper records of grades in folders. And, he says, he will continue to require his students to "write out in cursive writing" their term papers, knowing they will receive two grades—one for content, one for English.

"You have to be able to communicate or you're not going anywhere!"

6

Computers in Classrooms May Not Increase Learning

Michael Zwaagstra

Michael Zwaagstra is an education expert and high school teacher in Manitoba, Canada. He also serves on Steinbach, Manitoba's city council.

Despite their touted benefits, computers in the classroom may not always assist learning and may hinder it. Studies demonstrate that there may not be a link between higher academic achievement and more access to computers at schools. Additionally, although computers in classrooms at higher grades promote computer literacy, they are not necessary at earlier grades and can actually stunt younger students' grasp of basic math and reading skills. Finally, not all teachers will use computers, applications, and software effectively in the classroom; training them to use these technologies properly takes time and money and cannot be achieved through day-long sessions. It is strongly suggested that school budgets be balanced and not swing too far in favor of information technology.

Most people accept it as a given that in order to function in the 21st century one has to be at least moderately computer literate. Computers are everywhere and an increasing number of employers expect their workers to know how to use them. Because this trend shows no signs of abating, it makes sense to do everything possible to ensure that young people entering the workforce are computer literate. As not every family in Canada has access to a computer at home, it is seen as imperative that public schools give all students the opportunity to learn how to use a computer.

However, some have argued that schools have swung too far in this direction and are introducing students to computers at a much earlier age than necessary. It has been pointed out that many of our students are too dependent upon computers and that this dependence has come at the expense of other important skills—such as reading and basic math. While computer literacy is important, it should not displace a solid education in the basics.

In addition, it is important to consider the significant costs involved in providing computers in classrooms. School divisions in Manitoba spend a considerable amount of money on computers on an annual basis. Since computers rapidly become obsolete, upgrading and replacing computer systems occurs regularly. Because of the major expense involved, schools should ensure that computers are introduced at an age when students receive the maximum benefit from the money spent.

We must not delude ourselves into thinking that more computer use increases academic achievement.

Information Technology in Manitoba Schools

The Manitoba government identified information technology as a foundation area that needs to be developed in every subject area and grade. Information technology includes the following: computers and their peripherals, computer software, the Internet and electronic multimedia. If skill in this area were developed in every subject area and grade, this would mean that students in public schools should have access to computers starting in kindergarten. This indicates that the provincial government clearly envisions an ever-increasing presence of computers in public school classrooms.

School divisions appear to have taken this mandate seriously since slightly more than $26 million is spent annually on information technology in public schools. Across Canada, students now have more access to computers and the Internet than ever before. Nationwide, schools have a 5:1 ratio of students to computers and three out of four school-aged children regularly access the Internet. The push to expose students to computers at younger ages will result in an increase in these numbers.

While in the past schools provided computer education during a separate class in a specially designated computer lab, schools are now moving to integrate computers as part of regular curricular instruction. This means many schools are providing multiple computers in each classroom in order to facilitate this integration of computer technology with regular instruction. As a result, information technology has become a significant part of school division budgets in Manitoba.

Reasons for Concern

The provincial government should seriously consider whether the pendulum in favour of information technology has swung too far in one direction. There are many reasons school divisions should be cautious about increasing their emphasis on information technology education in regular classrooms.

1) Studies show that when factors such as household income are controlled, there is no evidence that greater access to computers at school has a positive correlation with academic achievement.

University of Munich economists Thomas Fuchs and Ludger Woessmann recently published a detailed analysis of the OECD Programme for International Student Assessment (PISA) standards tests. PISA is an international standardized assessment administered to fifteen-year-old students in over forty countries. Areas assessed by PISA include mathematical literacy, problem solving, reading literacy and scientific literacy.

Interestingly, Fuchs and Woessmann found that when controlled for variables such as household income, students with the most access to computers at home and school had lower scores in math, reading and science than did students with less computer access. While a moderate level of computer access had a positive correlation with student achievement, excessive computer access had a negative correlation. According to Fuchs and Woessmann, the "conditional relationship between student achievement and computer and internet use at school has an inverted U-shape"—meaning that schools need to guard against making unnecessary use of computers in classrooms.

A recently published study from Israel provides further evidence for the ineffectiveness of increasing the number of computers in schools. In 1994, the Israeli State Lottery sponsored the installation of a large number of computers in elementary and middle schools throughout the country. As a result, Israeli teachers reported that they significantly increased their computer-aided instruction (CAI) in the regular classroom. However, the increase in CAI did not translate into higher test scores. If additional computers in schools did make a difference in student learning, one would see different results in this study.

Computer technology is only a tool and is only useful if teachers know how to use it effectively.

Thus, while it may be reasonable to include a moderate amount of computer instruction in public schools, we must not delude ourselves into thinking that more computer use increases academic achievement.

2) Equipping schools with additional computers can be very expensive. Since school divisions have fixed budgets, money is often diverted from other important areas.

Computer technology is expensive. The $26 million [Canadian] spent annually on information technology in Manitoba school divisions represents almost 2 per cent of all educational expenditures in the province. Unlike most other capital expenditures, computers depreciate rapidly. It does not take long for computers purchased today to become obsolete. Obviously, if schools endeavour to provide a computer for each student, computer expenses can be expected to increase substantially on an annual basis. This money could be put to better use in other areas such as purchasing textbooks and upgrading school buildings.

3) While it may make sense for students in higher grades to become computer literate, the same does not hold true for those in earlier grades. Introducing computers at too young an age can have a negative effect on academic achievement.

Students in the early and middle years do not need to use computers to the same degree as those in the senior years. Thomas Fuchs, co-author of the previously mentioned study that showed a negative correlation between computer access and academic achievement, speculated that young children are even more damaged by excessive computer access than are the 15 year olds he tested as part of the PISA study. Since computer use often reduces pupil-teacher interaction, this could have a negative impact on literacy since the learning of reading requires extensive interaction between students and teachers.

In addition, since computer hardware and software rapidly become obsolete, it is difficult to see how requiring young students to become familiar with software that will be obsolete by the time they reach high school is beneficial to their academic learning. Their time would be better spent getting a solid grasp of the basics—such as reading and mathematics. If students have access to computers at school in grade 9, they will have plenty of time to become fully computer literate by the time they graduate from high school.

4) Not all teachers are skilled at integrating computer instruction into the regular classroom. Upgrading computer labs and providing students with personal laptops will be of little use if teachers are unable to effectively incorporate them into their instruction.

It should be noted that computer technology is simply a tool and is only useful if teachers know how to use it effectively. Not all teachers are equally computer literate and, considering the large number of teachers who are nearing retirement age, it is to be expected that many of them are not skilled at computer technology instruction. Unfortunately, school divisions often deal with this problem superficially by bringing in outside experts to provide daylong sessions on specific software programs. This is a woefully inadequate way to address this problem since people who are computer illiterate cannot become skilled computer users in a couple of prepackaged, daylong sessions. As a result, school divisions need to spend more time ensuring that staff members are fully computer literate before purchasing expensive computer systems for their students.

Rethinking the Emphasis on Information Technology

It is evident that the Manitoba government needs to seriously rethink its emphasis on information technology. While it is important for high school graduates to be computer literate, this does not translate into requiring students in grade 1 to make regular use of computers in the classroom. In fact, studies show that students with the most access to computers at home and school have lower test scores than those who have less access to computers. Many of these researchers believe that younger students are even more negatively affected by excessive computer exposure than are those in higher grades.

In addition, computer technology is very expensive and school divisions already spend more than $26 million [Canadian] per year in this area. Because computers rapidly become obsolete, it is costly to keep school computer labs up to date. It would be more effective for computer instruction to take place at the high school level rather than beginning at the early or middle levels. This way, teachers at the younger grade levels would be able to focus on providing a solid grounding in the basics so that their students are prepared for high school.

Students need to learn how to operate computers. However, the province needs to implement a more balanced information technology strategy in order to ensure that schools maintain a proper balance in this area. Information technology is *not* "a foundation skill area to be developed in every subject area and grade."

7

Online Classes Can Increase Learning

The Education Innovator

The Education Innovator *is the newsletter of the Office of Innovation and Improvement (OII), the U.S. Department of Education.*

A staggering percentage of American youths use the Internet and its applications on a regular basis to interact with one another. Therefore, appropriately integrating online classes with education can serve the needs of a wide spectrum of students. For example, the scheduling and pacing flexibility of online classes can help at-risk students graduate. Online classes also offer opportunities for students to enroll in advanced courses or specialized electives not taught at their schools due to the lack of qualified teachers or resources or scheduling conflicts. In today's information age, educators should work to end the "digital disconnect" between schools and the most Internet-savvy generation yet.

Kevin left school when his mom went to jail. He worked long hours to support himself, so he couldn't attend regular classes. After he moved in with a cousin who convinced him to try online courses, he thought he'd give it a try. Without school or parental support, he struggled to finish the online classes on time and to pass the exams, but he found support from teachers and the flexibility he needed through the virtual classroom, and he eventually earned his high school diploma.

The Education Innovator, "Welcome to the Cyber Classroom," vol. 6, February 29, 2008.

The fictional story above, which is based on a number of real-life accounts, demonstrates how online courses can meet the needs of many kinds of students, and why these courses are here to stay. Like Kevin, middle school and high school students are dropping out in record numbers. A recent report, *The Silent Epidemic: Perspectives of High School Dropouts*, found that "circumstances in students' lives and an inadequate response to those circumstances from the schools led to dropping out." Most students surveyed for the report said that their classes were uninteresting and lacked opportunities for "real world" learning, so the students lost interest in going to school. Other reasons that students dropped out included the need to make money, to care for a family member, to raise a child, or because academic challenges caused them to fail or fall behind due to a lack of earlier preparation.

Appropriately implemented, online learning can enable districts to provide solutions to help address each of these reasons students leave school and as a consequence, could play an important role in reducing the current rate of high school dropouts. A Project Tomorrow survey of more than 319,000 K-12 students nationwide discovered that 57 percent of high school students indicated interest in or have taken an online course in the past year, and 39 percent liked the self-pacing that online classes could provide. In 2007, the North American Council for Online Learning (NACOL) found that "42 states have significant supplemental online learning programs, or significant full-time programs, or both. Only eight states do not have either of these options, and several of these states have begun planning for online learning development."

The Growth of Online Learning

Teens are one of America's fastest growing groups of online users and consumers. Just six years ago, surveys showed that merely 60 percent of American school-aged children used the Internet. Yet as of November 2006, a PEW Internet & American Life Project survey showed a dramatic increase, with 93 percent of teenagers online regularly and more than nine in 10 Americans between the ages of 12 and 17 using the Internet. The fact is that more teens than ever before use the Internet as a way to interact with others—and it's not just to send and receive email, but to create and share information and content more often than any other age group in the country.

There is still a "digital disconnect" between schools and students.

While teens are immersed in the online culture, according to a 2007 survey by the Sloan Consortium, only 700,000 public school students, mostly high schoolers, enrolled in online courses in 2005–06. While the total number represents a very small sample of the total high school population, the latest Sloan figures represent a tenfold increase over the number enrolled in online courses over their survey in the year 2000, and that number is growing. A 2002–03 National for Education Statistics (NCES) report on distance learning found that an estimated 8,200 public schools had students enrolled in technology-based distance education courses, which represents 9 percent of all public schools nationwide. That survey revealed that the percentage of schools with students enrolled in distance education courses varied substantially by the instructional level of the school. Overall, 38 percent of public high schools offered distance education courses, compared with 20 percent of combined or ungraded schools, 4 percent of middle or junior high schools, and fewer than 1 percent of elementary schools.

While some schools do respond to and embrace this new teen culture, there is still a "digital disconnect" between schools and students. In the 2002 PEW Internet & American Life Project study, *The Digital Disconnect: The Widening Gap Between Internet-Savvy Students and Their Schools*, students revealed that the Internet helped them do their homework, and they described many other ways the Internet is used for education-related activities. Indeed, they use the Web as an "online textbook." They sift through reference materials, organize information, and study with friends through instant messaging. Students report, however, that there is a "substantial disconnect between how they use the Internet for school and how they use the Internet during the school day and under teacher direction." And even in the relatively small number of well-connected schools, students report that the quality of web-based assignments can be poor and uninspiring. Since then, there is increased acceptance of online curriculum, but many schools and teachers have not acknowledged that "online" is the way students communicate.

It is possible, nevertheless, to provide quality online learning opportunities that engage and inspire students. The number of online providers that utilize Internet technology to deliver effective, non-traditional learning approaches to students is growing, and several states are moving ahead with legislation that will offer online curricula as a practical alternative to the traditional classroom.

Challenging Students Outside the Classroom Walls

"Harnessing the power of innovation for the benefit of American schools is fast becoming an education imperative," said Secretary [Margaret] Spellings in the introduction to the newest OII Innovations in Education Guide, *Connecting Students to Advanced Courses Online.* The Guide, along with a webcast that promoted its availability this December [2007], focuses on case studies from six providers who offer rigorous curricula to students through the Web. The online content includes a variety of Advanced Placement (AP) courses, International Baccalaureate (IB) classes, and other dual enrollment options that enable students to earn college credit while still in high school.

The Guide gives examples of promising practices in key areas including ensuring course quality; recruiting, counseling, and supporting students; and tracking outcomes for continuous improvement. According to the introduction, the Guide's "aim is to familiarize districts and schools with the issues they must consider and address if students are to achieve success in this new form of learning." But students are ready to welcome the virtual classroom.

Jesse, a very bright student, who found many classes uninteresting, was energized by the idea of taking more advanced classes than offered at her high school, with the idea that she could graduate early and attend college. She is taking online AP Macroeconomics in the tenth grade. She chose online classes so she can challenge herself in ways she never thought possible.

Online education can help students succeed.

Motivated students such as Jesse, who are looking to expand their educational options, are just as likely to find online courses beneficial as students with academic challenges. Yet, according to the National Center for Education Statistics, advanced courses in English, mathematics, science, and foreign language are unavailable to as many as a quarter of high school students. Educators say there are various reasons schools cannot offer advanced classes—lack of qualified teachers, low student interest, and students' scheduling conflicts are the most common. Online courses are one way to help overcome these barriers and bridge the gap.

Florida Virtual School—An Example of a Program that Serves a Range of Students

One of the providers featured in the guide, Florida Virtual School (FLVS), serves students who are prepared for and interested in enrolling in AP courses and those who might benefit from a virtual classroom because of their special circumstances. Florida law requires that priority for age and grade appropriate classes be given to students from schools that are rural, low-performing, high-minority, and home- or hospital-bound students. Thanks to state funding, FLVS classes are free for all Florida students and open to non-Florida residents who pay a nominal fee.

FLVS offers a range of online courses and tools, including the following: 11 AP courses; core academic courses such as English and mathematics; online preparation classes for Florida's statewide assessments; SAT preparation courses; and AP exam reviews. Since its inception in 1997, when it offered just five classes serving 77 students, FLVS has continued to grow. It now offers more than 85 classes serving over 31,000 students.

Most recently, they have added a middle school program that will have regular and accelerated classes. According to one educator, "Adding middle school online courses partners very nicely with the opportunities to offer middle school students pre-AP level courses. In our experience with the online Advanced Placement, you really need to work with students at the middle school level with some kind of course that's going to excite them about advanced coursework and engage them in curriculum that they are going to need to succeed in AP at the high school level."

Students and parents are enthusiastic about their experiences with FLVS. One parent said that FLVS "was the best thing to ever happen to my son's life. . . . It saved at least one kid from being lost in the system. He probably would have dropped out." Another parent said that FLVS has filled a need for them because, due to her husband's job, they live in a rural area that doesn't have the advanced courses her child needed, and the online school "allows us to stay together as a family a lot more than if she were enrolled in the local high school full-time." Another student said, "I am currently taking Marine Science Honors through the Florida Virtual School, as well as going to [my local] high school. The Virtual School is a great institution. It has allowed me to take extra courses, and now I can graduate a year early. This program has been a tremendous help to me."

Teachers at FLVS are dedicated and engaged, collaborating from different content areas in teams known as "schoolhouses." They share perspectives about teaching so that others can gather new ideas and creatively improve their own methods. FLVS employs 425 full-time and 200 part-time state certified instructors, boasting a 95 percent teacher retention rate.

Online education can help students succeed, giving them opportunities to take advanced courses, to take more interesting courses than those offered at their local school, or simply to provide the challenge and incentive to stay in school. They serve an important purpose in today's information age, and there is no doubt that delivering coursework over the Internet is a development whose time has come.

8

Online Classes Should Be Used Moderately

Karen Nitkin

Karen Nitkin is a Maryland-based writer and contributor to the Baltimore Sun.

Online courses offer numerous advantages: students, parents, and educators are attracted to their flexibility, and they offer students the opportunity to take courses not available at their schools. However, online education is not a replacement for teaching in traditional classrooms and should be limited. Face-to-face interaction is critical to learning, and it is not advisable that any student receive all of his or her education online and outside of the classroom. Furthermore, some virtual schools are troubling because they are operated by for-profit businesses, with many of their home-schooled students being instructed by their parents, not certified instructors.

Jessica Brown, a junior at West Chester East High School in West Chester, Pennsylvania, decided to challenge herself this year by taking Advanced Placement biology.

Small problem, though. Her school didn't offer the course, a demanding college-level walk through the mysteries of DNA and photosynthesis.

Not to worry. Brown discovered the Massachusetts-based Virtual High School, which offers the course over the Web and added her to its growing roster of students who meet

Karen Nitkin, "Login and Learn," *NEA Today*, May 2005. Reproduced by permission of the National Education Association. www.nea.org/neatoday/0505/onlineed.html.

teacher (and classmates) online. Brown's "virtual" instructor, Laura Hajdukiewicz, teaches science at Andover High School in Massachusetts, but she could just as easily hail from the other side of the country.

Under the Virtual High School system, teachers like Hajdukiewicz lead one class online for students anywhere in the world, and in exchange, 25 students can take online classes and receive credit at their own schools.

While the vast majority of K-12 students continue to attend classes in traditional bricks-and-mortar schools, more are taking one or two courses from a growing list of providers like the Virtual High School, a nonprofit organization that offers more than 200 courses.

It's a system that increasing numbers of educators and students find attractive indeed. Recently, the National Center for Education Statistics reported that enrollments in distance education courses (which include both Web-based courses and older technologies such as two-way interactive video hookups) in public K-12 schools topped 327,000 in the 2002–03 school year. In urban and suburban districts, online courses have surpassed video programming as the top method of distance learning.

Even supporters of online education are troubled by the growth of "cyber-charters."

Flexibility a Plus

Advocates of distance learning say online courses, though not a replacement for traditional classrooms, offer some pluses.

Flexible scheduling tops the list, says Bruce Friend, chief administrative officer for the Florida Virtual High School, which has seen enrollment jump from 77 students when it launched in 1996–97 to more than 18,000 students this year. Many high achievers, especially in small districts, may be ready to take advanced or specialized courses their local schools simply don't provide, Friend points out. Other students take a course online because they need to make up a class, or their overstuffed schedules require them to take classes outside regular school hours. "One of my first students was very involved in student government and in band, and he was on the soccer team," says Friend, who taught before taking the administrative position. "And—oh yeah—he needed to take U.S. government in order to graduate." By taking the course online, "he was able to do them all."

Ruth Adams, a former teacher and contract negotiator for the Massachusetts Teachers Association who now serves as dean of students at the Virtual High School, believes that students taking courses online hone their ability to work independently and manage their time. Students in regular classes learn these skills, too, but when you're taking a Web-based class, "There's nobody standing over you making you sit down and do your work," she says.

Teaching over the Internet is challenging, but Hajduk-iewicz is creative about finding substitutes for hands-on lab work. Her students do a virtual pig dissection instead of the real thing, and learn to classify cells without looking through a microscope. "Doing it online is not going to give them the same experience, but for some students it's the best they've got," she says.

Steady Does It

Kids and teachers who take advantage of this virtual learning are definitely connected—by their mouses and Internet hook-ups—but are they really, well, connected?

While supportive of distance learning's potential to expand opportunities for students and staff, a 2002 NEA [National Education Association] policy statement notes that face-to-face opportunities are critical, too. NEA's statement advised against arrangements in which students "receive all or most of their education at home through distance education and rarely convene in an actual school building."

Even supporters of online education are troubled by the growth of "cyber-charters." These are virtual schools that students attend full time, under existing state laws for charter schools. Some of the schools are run by for-profit businesses; many of the customers are home-schooled kids taught by their parents, rather than a certified instructor, notes Barbara Stein, a technology expert with NEA.

Schools such as the Massachusetts-based Virtual High School, though, use certified teachers with special training in online delivery, and they take steps to ensure that students stay connected. Unless there are exceptional circumstances, students are limited to two online courses per semester, says Adams. And Hajdukiewicz says that online courses "are more interactive than many believe." Her students cooperate on lab work, work on presentations together, and have "heated debates" that transcend distance.

Before Christmas break, Hajdukiewicz faced one of the toughest tests of classroom community: One of her cyberstudents, Angie, was killed in a car accident. She had to break the news to her other pupils by posting an announcement on the class page, and she created a discussion thread so students could reflect and react. Though separated by distance, the kids bonded. Said one student's post: "Reading about Angie really slowed down the cadence of life, and made me appreciate many of the smaller things. Until now, I guess I thought of everybody (including myself) as a name on a list. . . . [B]ut Angie's death has made the entire class so much more human to me." Adds Hajdukiewicz, "That definitely made the class seem more real to me as well."

9

The Internet Can Increase Learning

Steve O'Hear

Steve O'Hear is a fellow at the National Endowment for Science, Technology, and the Arts (NESTA) in the United Kingdom and a journalist and technology consultant.

Though the Internet has revolutionized commerce, media, and business, its potential as a learning tool has yet to be embraced in education. Students can use blogs to break down the barriers of traditional publishing and facilitate discussions with teachers, classmates, and wide audiences. Podcasts are also gaining in popularity in schools—it is both a source of educational digital content and a hands-on activity when students produce their own podcasts. Photosharing sites, such as Flickr, are virtual libraries of images students can use for presentations as well as a platform for them to share their photographs, and students can use YouTube to air self-produced video clips. These Web tools and services enhance education and empower students.

Much has been written on *Read/WriteWeb* (and elsewhere) about the effect that web technologies are having on commerce, media, and business in general. But outside of the 'edublogosphere', there's been little coverage of the impact it is having on education. Teachers are starting to explore the potential of blogs, media-sharing services and other social software—which, although not designed specifically for e-learning, can be used to empower students and create exciting new learning opportunities.

Steve O'Hear, "E-learning 2.0—How Web Technologies Are Shaping Education," ReadWriteWeb.com, August 8, 2006. Reproduced by permission. www.readwriteweb.com/archives/e-learning_20.php.

As I wrote in *The Guardian* [in 2005]: "Like the web itself, the early promise of e-learning—that of empowerment—has not been fully realized. The experience of e-learning for many has been no more than a hand-out published online, coupled with a simple multiple-choice quiz. Hardly inspiring, let alone empowering. But by using these new web services, e-learning has the potential to become far more personal, social and flexible."

Blogging is increasingly finding a home in education.

The traditional approach to e-learning has been to employ the use of a Virtual Learning Environment (VLE), software that is often cumbersome and expensive—and which tends to be structured around courses, timetables, and testing. That is an approach that is too often driven by the needs of the institution rather than the individual learner. In contrast, e-learning 2.0 (as coined by [information technology expert] Stephen Downes) takes a 'small pieces, loosely joined' approach that combines the use of discrete but complementary tools and web services—such as blogs, wikis, and other social software—to support the creation of ad-hoc learning communities.

Blogging

Blogging is increasingly finding a home in education (both in school and university), as not only does the software remove the technical barriers to writing and publishing online—but the 'journal' format encourages students to keep a record of their thinking over time. Blogs also of course facilitate critical feedback, by letting readers add comments—which could be from teachers, peers or a wider audience.

Students use of blogs [is] far ranging. A single authored blog can be used to provide a personal space online, to pose questions, publish work in progress, and link to and comment on other web sources. However a blog needn't be limited to a single author—it can mix different kinds of voices, including fellow students, teachers and mentors, or subject specialists. Edu-blogging pioneer Will Richardson (author of a book entitled *Blogs, Wikis, Podcasts and Other Powerful Web Tools for Classrooms*) used the blog software Manila to enable his English literature students to publish a readers guide to the book *The Secret Life of Bees*. Richardson asked the book's author, Sue Monk Kidd, if she would participate by answering questions and commenting on what the students had written—to which she agreed. The result was a truly democratic learning space.

More Edu-blogging Examples

Under the guidance of [teacher and social networking expert] Ewan McIntosh, Musselburgh Grammar School in Scotland has, for the second year running, published a travel blog of the school's annual trip to Paris and Normandy (using TypePad's hosted blogging service). Additionally, the student council publishes a blog to keep the school's community informed and involved on various issues. McIntosh has also pioneered the use of Podcasting in education (more below), and last year, the school's MGS Podcast was short-listed for a New Statesman New Media award.

School children in the UK are proof that you're never too young to start edu-blogging. Inspired by their teacher John Mills, the seven year-old students at West Blatchington School in Hove blog fanatically. The school even holds blogging assemblies, as I found out when I had the privilege of meeting the next generation of bloggers for a film I presented [in 2005] for Teacher's TV.

Teachers who are subject specialists are also using blogs to provide up-to-date information and commentary on their subject areas, as well as posting questions and assignments and linking to relevant news stories and websites. Media studies teacher Pete Fraser runs one such blog (using Blogger) for his students at Long Road sixth-form college, in Cambridge, UK.

Inevitably, educationalists are also using blogs to share their innovative use of web 2.0 in education—and, in turn, spread good practice. Prominent UK edu-bloggers that I'm subscribed to (aside from those already mentioned) include Josie Fraser, Miles Berry, Peter Ford and Terry Freedman.

Podcasting

Podcasting has become a popular technology in education, in part because it provides a way of pushing educational content to learners. For example, Stanford University has teamed up with Apple to create the Stanford iTunes University—which provides a range of digital content (some closed and some publicly accessible) that students can subscribe to using Apple's iTunes software.

However, student-produced podcasts are where it's at when it comes to educational podcasting. Swap 'user-generated content' for 'learner-generated content' and you soon get the picture. Apple, with its strong presence in the education market, has been quick to recognize the learning potential of student podcasting. Apple is heavily marketing its iPod and associated content creation tools (iMovie, GarageBand, and iTunes) to the education sector. The podcasting section of iTunes even has a category dedicated to education.

For a great example of a student-produced podcast, check out the MGS Podcast which I wrote about for *The Guardian*. As with blogging, podcasting provides students with a sense of audience—and they are highly motivated to podcast because the skills required seem 'relevant' to today's world.

Media Sharing

The photo-sharing site Flickr is also finding use within education—as it provides, a valuable resource for students and educators looking for images for use in presentations, learning materials or coursework. Many of the images uploaded to Flickr carry a Creative Commons license, making them particularly suitable for educational use—and the tagging of images makes it much easier to find relevant content.

Students can also use Flickr to publish their digital photography to a wider audience. And like blogging, the commenting function on Flickr allows for critical feedback. A lesser-known feature of Flickr—the ability to add hot-spot annotations to an image—also has much potential as a learning tool. Beth Harris, director of distance learning at the Fashion Institute of Technology, State University of New York, has used this feature to enable her students to annotate and discuss a series of paintings as part of an online art history course.

Pete Fraser (mentioned above) has been experimenting with the use of video-sharing site YouTube with his media studies students, as part of a course on new media. Rather than have students prepare a traditional presentation, students were asked to produce a short video on a chosen new media subject—examples included MySpace and the rise of the iPod. Videos were then published onto YouTube, where they can be viewed and commented on by classmates and the wider YouTube community.

DOPA and Social Networks

The educational potential of social software and services is huge. However, much of the work being done by educators (of which I've barely scratched the surface) is in danger of being undermined by the recently proposed Deleting Online Predators Act (DOPA). This legislation [not yet enacted as of April 2008] attempts to address the moral panic over sites like MySpace and the perceived 'dangers' they pose to children, by banning the use of commercial social networking websites in

US schools and libraries which receive federal IT funding. A "commercial social networking website" is defined as any web service that:

> ". . . allows users to create web pages or profiles that provide information about themselves and are available to other users; and offers a mechanism for communication with other users, such as a forum, chat room, email, or instant messenger."

10

The Internet Can Disrupt Learning

Tim Lougheed

Tim Lougheed is president of the Canadian Science Writers' Association and a writer specializing in science, medicine, and education.

The Internet has many merits as an educational tool, but it can be a disruptive presence in the classroom. During lectures, discussions, or class presentations, students using laptops may be distracted by surfing on the Internet or instant messaging with classmates or friends, leaving instructors and presenters to compete for students' attention. Consequently, as schools increase the availability of wireless Internet in classrooms and offices and encourage or require students to own laptops, they must balance the advantages offered by the Internet with "chalk talk" and foster the student–teacher relationship. Allowing students to access the Internet in the classroom also calls for a new electronic etiquette for them to follow in respect for instructors.

When Mala Thakoor was doing her BA at York University in the early 1990s, the Web and its associated applications were just beginning to make their presence felt. The idea of introducing this new technology into a classroom would not have occurred to most instructors, unless perhaps they were teaching a specialized course in computer science. Nor would it have occurred to most students to demand it.

Now an administrative assistant with York's Centre for the Support of Teaching, Ms. Thakoor returned to classroom this

Tim Lougheed, "The Internet as a Class Distraction," *University Affairs*, January 2002, pp. 26–28. Reproduced by permission.

fall to begin arts course in multimedia design, and was surprised at how much had changed. The class took place in a computer lab with each student at a separate workstation, linked to the others through an internal network as well as to the Internet. The arrangement allowed students to examine computer-generated images and share their own graphics work with other members of the class.

Ms. Thakoor discovered that the presence of computers also carried some unintended consequences. The instructor had to compete for students' attention as they e-mailed messages to one another or surfed the Web. After repeatedly asking them to look his way, he ordered everyone to turn their chairs away from their monitors. "It took at lot of prying." says Ms. Thakoor. "They were so hesitant to leave their terminals."

None of this was new to Don Sinclair, the York faculty of fine arts instructor who has been teaching multimedia courses using the Internet in class since 1990. The subject matter makes computer labs the ideal classroom for this course, and over the years he has seen students become much more comfortable in this computer-intensive setting. So much so, in fact, that their distraction has become one of his leading challenges. "You have to explicitly say 'please look at me'," he observes. "Because if they have the computer in front of them, the keyboards and the mice will be clicking."

At the request of complaining instructors, some classrooms have been outfitted with "kill switches" that temporarily disconnect a classroom's data ports from Internet access.

Instructors who have to meet this challenge remain the exception rather than the rule in most Canadian post secondary institutions, but the mesmerizing power of information technology is intruding on more classrooms than ever before. Distance education facilities, for example, often rely on connecting two or more remote sites using the Internet. Computers have been finding their way into many traditional lecture theatres or seminar rooms, with a monitor sprouting at each desk. In other cases, such as Mr. Sinclair's multimedia course, there are advantages to having students linked to a local network to work on a common piece of software or view a common set of images. In a number of academic programs, students are expected to supply their own laptop computers and each seat will have an independent port to connect them to the network.

In the U.S., business schools that have invested a great deal of effort and expense to embrace this technology are now finding they have to set rules to curtail the distractions it's causing in class. At the request of complaining instructors, some classrooms have been outfitted with "kill switches" that temporarily disconnect a classroom's data ports from Internet access. This technically complicated response may not yet have been deemed necessary on Canadian campuses, but instructor complaints can be heard there, too.

Among them is McMaster University sociology professor Carl Cuneo, director of the Network for the Evaluation of Education and Training Technologies, a national research consortium that examines issues such as the role of the Internet in teaching. His own perspective was shaped by an experience with a distance education course that was held in a computer lab to allow remote members of the class to take part in the proceedings online. When he asked those students to make presentations to the rest of the class, he encountered many of the same frustrations as Mr. Sinclair.

"Other students were at their terminals and they had open chat lines," he says. "During the presentations the other students were chatting with one another, making snide remarks about the student doing the presentation. They were also engaged in all kinds of other socializing and surfing the Net. This had nothing to do with the presentation. This clearly was an inappropriate atmosphere."

The Perennial Challenges of Classroom Etiquette

Of course, students were finding ways of distracting themselves in the classroom long before the Internet showed up, and teachers have always had to cope with individuals who chat in class, pass notes to one another or read comics behind a strategically positioned textbook. Christopher Knapper, director of Queen's University's Instructional Development Centre, suggest this new technology has merely added another dimension to these perennial challenges of classroom etiquette. It has always been up to instructors to meet those challenges, he says, preferably with more imaginative measures than an "off" switch for the Web.

Dr. Knapper says the most successful instructors are able to engage a student's interest. "What you're seeing with students who are surfing the Web is that you have provided another possible source of engagement, another source of attention," he says. "You're competing with that. If you don't have engagement, you don't have attention. If you don't have attention, you don't really have learning."

Some modest debate over the presence of the Internet in classrooms surfaced at Queen's four years ago [in 1998], when its school of business quietly launched a program to incorporate student laptops into more teaching activities. But Brent Gallupe, one of the professors responsible for the initiative, says instructors at Queen's have seldom encountered the serious problems that have dogged their counterparts south of the border. "We're still learning what works and what doesn't," he says.

What works for him is presenting students with a set of straightforward guidelines, including rules such as "tops down'"—laptops closed when they are not needed for class-room activities. Such rules reflect standards of behaviour that prospective business people might be expected to follow in the working world. But Dr. Gallupe has a more important distinction in mind. "I view the class and the classroom sessions as a compilation of human moments and technology moments," he says.

That distinction sits well with Maurice Tugwell. assistant dean of arts at Acadia University. For more than five years, his campus has been on the front lines of writing classrooms and dealing with the consequences. Every student is now required to own a laptop, and access ports for linking them to the Internet are in every nook and cranny. Classrooms, residence rooms and library carrels are only the most obvious of those locations. Hallway kiosks make it possible to log on without even sitting down. Students bring their computers to surf together over a pitcher of beer in the pub. Professors' offices now feature extra ports next to their desks, so that students can set up their laptops during a visit.

Dr. Tugwell regards himself as typical of Acadia instructors who have tried to strike a balance between taking advantage of computers in some teaching situations and ignoring them in others. For instance, he finds it helpful to have the students use their laptops to work out complex exercises or case studies during a statistics course that he teaches. In other cases, he finds it more useful to resort to "chalk talk", the time-tested approach of lecturing and writing on a blackboard. He finds it revealing that chalk talk dominates an executive MBA course he teaches, though his students there are among the most ardent laptop users to be found anywhere.

"Many of them are much more technologically precocious than I am, but interestingly enough we don't use the laptops, because we have so much material to cover in such a short period time," he says. "I find it's more effective to give them reading assignments in advance and then hit the high spots."

In 30 years of teaching, Dr. Tugwell has witnessed the ebb and flow of various teaching technologies. The most recent innovations associated with the computer have presented him with many new opportunities as well as some new problems. On the one hand, he is not above treating students to a little Dire Straits or Pink Floyd before class starts, played through his laptop over the high-quality speakers that have been installed in many Acadia lecture halls. By the same token, he now has to cope with inadvertent disruptions such as the one caused by a student's Pamela Anderson screen saver.

Technical staff at Acadia bristle at the idea that such problems might inspire an instructor to ask for Internet access to be temporarily denied to a particular classroom. While not impossible, the procedure is complicated, and staff members have better things to do with their time. For professors who find themselves having difficulties coping with the Web in their classes, the recommended course is to deal with the classes first and Web afterward.

Moreover, Jacques Nantel a marketing professor at Montreal's École des Hautes Études Commerciales, adds that even the supposedly definitive solution of an "off" switch could prove futile. HEC introduced a program that made laptops universally required by students in many programs, and many of the models used by students can establish a wireless link with the Internet. Regardless of whether the data ports in the classroom are available, this hardware makes it possible to dial up the network in much the same way as using a cellular phone.

From Screen to Screen

In fact, the University of Western Ontario's Richard Ivey School of Business installed wireless Internet links in its classrooms. The move eliminated the expense of running wiring through the floors and walls of the school's older buildings. It also showed many instructors what could lie ahead: classrooms occupied by students using laptops—or even more discreet hand-held computers—linked to the Internet regardless of whether the classroom itself had any visible telecommunications nodes.

That prospect doesn't bother Acadia's Dr. Tugwell, whose students continue to find it productive and more rewarding to interact with him in much the same way as he has done for decades. In his specialty course on environmental economics, he sticks to the tried and true.

"I only use a laptop there for a special presentation, or to take students to Web sites that might be interesting," he says. "I use it much more out of class as a communications device or discussion device. There are only 30 [students] in the class, and if they're really interested in the class, then we should be talking to each other. I don't like the notion of talking to them from my screen to their screen."

He also resents the popularity of software such as Power-Point, which presents too much information in too stilted a fashion. Professor Tugwell urges instructors to avoid bombarding their students in this way, just for the sake of using new technology. At the same time, he reminds them that resources like the Web always deserve a fair trial, since they can bring exciting features to teaching and learning.

"I really embraced it in the sense that I have a healthy respect for it, as a substitute and a complement, depending on the circumstances," he says. "It will never replace the relationship you have with fellow humans in this journey with your students."

11

Social Networking Can Increase Learning

Ewan McIntosh

Ewan McIntosh is a national adviser on learning and technology futures for Learning and Teaching Scotland. He is also a speaker and consultant on social networking.

Social networking is arriving in schools and will transform educational methods for the greater good. It takes learning beyond the classroom and engages students by fostering interaction and social exchange with each other, allowing them to publish and comment on each other's work on a vastly greater scale. Social networking also promotes learning as an experience that emphasizes collaboration and communication rather than the passive absorption of information through books and chalkboard teaching, linking students to a network of teachers and a myriad of political, economic, and cultural views. Young students have an inherent ability for social networking; therefore, fusing the technology with education is approrpriate.

Proposition: This house believes that social networking technologies will bring large positive changes to educational methods, in and out of the classroom.

It predicts a future of learning through screens, a world where the cyborg provides the information and students don't even have to remember anything, thanks to their memory chips, implanted at birth. I imagine, though, that in that infomercial there is still some form of school building, grouping those who come from a geographically similar location and similar age.

Social networking in all its forms has already begun to transform the way teachers teach, learners learn and education managers lead learning, and will continue to do so.

Humans have, over the years, been pitiful at predicting the scale of things to come.

Predictions like these have been surpassed by something far more powerful and awe-inspiring, if not yet completely accepted by the education Establishment: social networking in all its forms has already begun to transform the way teachers teach, learners learn and education managers lead learning, and will continue to do so.

Social networking has arrived in hundreds of thousands of classrooms and is attempting to show that technology in education is less about anonymous chips and bytes filling up our children with knowledge, less about teachers reinforcing a 'chalk and talk' style with an interactive whiteboard, and less about death by PowerPoint bullets. It's more about helping learners become more world-aware, more communicative, learning from each other, understanding first hand what makes the world go around.

In Scotland, I've been fortunate to work with thousands of school children and hundreds of teachers, creating mini social networks based around a rather traditional 'social object': the classroom. Students have been empowered to publish not just their best work, but the many drafts it takes to get there. They've received feedback from 'real' people outside school and, surprisingly often, the occasional expert has paid a visit (my personal favourite: the professional diver that corrected one student ended up being invited to visit the school to demonstrate the various bits of kit that go into a marine biology dive).

Importantly, they've received more communication, feedback and interest from the one group they value most: their parents. Parents, too, have reported feeling more in touch with what their children are actually learning, rather than simply what they've 'done' at school that day. Teachers feel more connection to parents, too, as communication is daily online, rather than once a year at parents' evenings.

It's true that for many school children, though, teaching methods have not really changed much since their parents were at school. It's going to take time for what the most bleeding edge teachers are doing to become the norm. But that's why this motion is spot on: since so many teachers have already made an impact on attainment and student learning experience through their use of social networks, exponential adoption of the 'new web' is only round the corner.

An impact of social networks on educational methods will happen . . . providing a learning experience that is accessible to all.

And even if it's not happening in schools, learning is about far more than what happens behind the school gate. Lifelong learning is the policy du jour, and rightly so. We are all learners, all the time. Ubiquitous social technologies help us connect to those who can help us learn when we're outside the domain of formal education. One of the biggest iTunes success stories this past year has been *Coffee Break* Spanish, run by a teacher from his home in a seaside town on the West of Scotland. "You've got Spanish native speakers learning French with *Coffee Break French*, helping out those from around the world learning Spanish on the *Coffee Break Spanish* blog," says Mark Pentleton, the 'teacher' whose 21st century remit is closer to that of a living breathing social network for a band of young and old learners of foreign languages.

The Bebo-boomer Generation

The web turned sixteen [in 2007], just as another generation of sixteen year olds left school with more knowledge of the web from outside formal education than from within it. This trend of learning about the potential of the web from outside the school gates will continue into the future, especially as social networks become ever more portable and mobile, on cell phones and gaming consoles, such as the highly pocketable Nintendo DS or Sony PSP.

Educational methods could continue on their merry, Victorian way, but that's unlikely to engage today's learners, and it's impossible to envisage tomorrow's parents, the Bebo Boomers, accepting the 9AM–4PM, timetabled, do the exams you're told to when you're told to, inflexibility of the 20th Century school. An impact of social networks on educational methods will happen, if not down to parent pressure alone but to kneel at the non-negotiable altar of Inclusion, that is, providing a learning experience that is accessible to all.

And so we come to the final part of those sixties' predictions, which always seemed to include a school building, not vastly different those our Victorian ancestors frequented. Even this is affected by social networking. In every developed country on the planet, and many developing nations, too, school design is top of the pile of educational reform. Yet social networking technology brings into question the very need for a building at all. When we consider the most successful school systems of the world and what makes them great, time in the school building is not one of them, but time learning is. In Singapore, where it's perfectly normal for a 'small' primary school building to have 1000 or more students, learning 'at school' takes place in two sittings, separated by lunch. But this does not mean learning stops. Take the examples of students in Perth, Scotland, who started publishing and peer-reviewing their extensive travel logs from a trip to the battlefields of World War One. On Bebo. After the school day was over. Educational methods will change to take advantage of this passion for extending learning out of hours.

Increasingly, as one baby boom generation of education leaders retires, the 'Bebo-boomer' generation takes up the helm of educational leadership. This is the generation who have a working understanding of the networked world, having used social networks and mobile computing seamlessly for years in their personal lives. Marrying their inbuilt capacity with social networks to the theory of sound educational practice, they will publish what they've been up to in their lessons, what went well and what didn't work out. They are used to others commenting on their work and, with this large-scale socially networked approach to teacher coaching, they will be more capable than today's unnetworked teachers to discern the good advice from the bad and act on it to improve their practice.

And, if you need a final point to consider, something practical to show the power of the social network for changing the way teachers learn themselves, just re-read this debate. It was written one Sunday afternoon, with collaboration over Twitter, the mobile phone and web-based social networking tool, with teaching colleagues, from the US, Scotland, Canada, England, France, New Zealand and Australia. Has social networking changed the face of educational methods? Almost certainly: yes.

Collaboration and Communication

We have all enjoyed the ability to talk publicly about these issues with someone else, someone we may not even know. We've enjoyed the insights from others, we've enjoyed learning from each other.

We have networked and learned from it.

It's also been fascinating to observe to-ing and fro-ing around our expectations of education in 2008, many of which fall far short of what current educational research shows as our most promising opportunities for improvement. Social networking's capacity to change educational methods for the better is undermined not only by differing understandings of the very tools and practices online, but by the underlining pedagogy that we are expecting to see in our classrooms. The discussions have revealed an almost submissive approach to effecting change, whether we are teachers, researchers, parents or students, blaming lack of change on something else, whether that be politics or assessment protocols.

The concepts of assessment for learning, particularly the value of peer- and self-assessment of work coupled with explicit, written-down or recorded logs of learning, are not recognized as a valuable norm in, arguably, the majority of our planet's classrooms. This, despite seminal research published ten years ago ([education experts Paul] Black and [Dylan] Wiliam's "Inside the Black Box") and world league table-beating countries using these practices showing otherwise. Futurelab's social media research shows that it's not only the communication and connections created but also the creation of new media for that communication that adds value to the educational method. 'Self reporting' via podcast led to 76% of students working better with each other than before, 65% better at understanding problems and 59% becoming better at communicating ideas.

Collaboration and communication help us understand the world around us better than simply sucking up information from one-way sources such as the textbook and chalk-and-talk teacher. Ultimately, we're already seeing that learning 'in the classroom' is, in the big scheme of educational methodology, playing second fiddle to learning outside the classroom, learning from experience.

Lifelong learning is the policy du jour, and a worthy one at that. Today's citizens, let alone tomorrow's ones, have to learn about learning above all. Those who remain dependent on the traditional unnetworked information-delivery world of learning will manage, if they're lucky, just to survive. In order to understand politics, business, other cultures and other points of view it seems almost imperative that we are not dependent on what our high school teacher or university lecturer told us. We need to have a lifelong set of peer-teachers on whom we can rely to thrive and social networks provide that ever-changing network of peers.

Simply using the Web as a postman to deliver innumerable PDFs and video lectures is not enough. Learners crave more interaction with those sharing their interest.

Rightly, my opponent worries about where the basics of this networked renaissance are going to come from. Social networks of the commercial variety, that is Facebook, Bebo, Ning et al., may have a place in those countries where it is unlikely that millions will be spent on Government-sponsored social networks of the kind we see in Scotland. Increasingly, social networks around cell phone technology will be more useful for much of the developing world, as well as many developed countries, where mobile technology is streaks ahead of wired internet.

The whole notion of trust and expertise has once more been thrust into the limelight, with several commenters unsure of this debater's 'expertise' to provide worthwhile substance on the issue at hand. Whether information is justifiable, correct or worthwhile clearly has an impact on whether social networking's inevitable influence on educational methods will be a positive or a negative one.

While comment is free, information is sacred. Cue the growing ranks of top universities and hoards of school teachers who freely share their resources, teaching and learning research and lesson ideas on the web. Thousands of lifelong learners are already taking to free course materials being offered on the web, courses at MIT Open Courseware or Open Yale. Information looks likely to remain sacred.

An Accelerating Effect

But simply using the web as a postman to deliver innumerable PDFs and video lectures is not enough. Learners crave more interaction with those sharing their interest. Distance learning courses have long been trying to replicate the social buzz of the post-lecture coffee shop or library chatter, and increasingly their portals resemble elements of our Facebooks, Flickrs, MySpaces and blogs. It's not that the chatter need change or misrepresent the facts, but that the conversation and connections help ground new learning in our minds.

Making social connections around learning is not a new idea, though social networks mean it takes less time and, given the potential for reaching around the globe for these networks, the difference in background of those involved can be refreshingly wide.

All of this might seem to fundamentally undermine traditional schooling, when the most worthwhile interactions appear only to happen online. We are certainly beginning to challenge the notion of a classroom that was set up over 100 years ago in the light of an industrial revolution, that required vast numbers of people to be filled up with knowledge to be thrown into the workplace quickly, the smokestack school in more than one sense. But this notion has indeed been challenged for far longer than online social networks have been around, but little change—incremental or radical—is reaching into classroom practice.

There is hope, though: social networks have started to have an accelerating effect on the practical implementation of the ideas originally published by the Ivan Illiches of this world, through the online actions and interactions of a growing innovative band of social networking school-builders, curriculum designers, teachers, parents and students.

It is worth remembering that, within the constraints and readership of The Economist.com, we are not tackling the billions on this small planet whose most basic "classroom education" barely exists, for whom social networking is not just a vague term, but an unknown one. My hope for the future is that these children will receive an education that has learnt from our mistakes, our arguments and our successes, and that we might indeed learn from their progress. Thankfully, these far more fundamental changes are likely to occur faster than they could have done even five years ago, with the digital breadcrumbs of all our journeys available and openly questionable in the months and years to come.

12

Social Networking Can Disrupt Learning

Anita Ramasastry

Anita Ramasastry is an associate professor of law at the University of Washington School of Law in Seattle. She is also a director of the Shidler Center for Law, Commerce and Technology.

While social networking is a boon to students in many ways, these sites can also create disruption at school when students engage in cyberbullying or post threatening or critical remarks about other students or school staff and faculty. Furthermore, some students post photographs depicting themselves violating the law or engaging in risque behavior. Nonetheless, the First Amendment shields the free speech of public school students and may actually protect the hostile or critical statements of others they post on social networks or blogs if off-campus computers and networks are used. Only when the postings "materially disrupt school activities" can public schools punish students—but not with consistent success; the First Amendment to the U.S. Constitution raises complicated legal issues around free speech.

The past few years have seen the growth of popular social networking websites for students: Three prominent examples are MySpace.com, Facebook.com, and Xanga.com. And within and outside such sites, student blogging, too, is wildly

Anita Ramasastry, "Can Schools Punish Students for Posting Offensive Content on MySpace and Similar Sites? Often the Answer Is No, Unless the Posting Materially Disrupts School Activities," Findlaw.com, May 1, 2006. Reproduced by permission. http://writ.news.findlaw.com/ramasastry/20060501.html.

popular: About four million teens—19% of 12- to 17-year olds who use the Internet—have created some sort of blog, according to a November 2005 Pew Internet & American Life Project study.

Unfortunately, however, such sites and blogs—despite all the good they've done for some students—have also created serious problems for other students, educators and even law enforcement. No wonder, then, that many schools have blocked students from accessing such sites while on campus.

Students need to remember that the law applies in cyberspace too: Threats and harassment are just as illegal online as offline. Defamation or libel can occur on the Internet as well as in a printed newspaper. And when it comes to evidence of crime, the content of a personal website may be even more damning, in some cases, than a fingerprint.

But what about instances when student postings on networking sites aren't illegal, nor do they evidence or enable a crime—but, nevertheless, the postings upset school administrators or faculty?

In such cases, as I will explain, the First Amendment [to the U.S. Constitution] will protect many student postings, as long as they do not "materially disrupt" school activities—and as long as the students attend public, not private, schools.

MySpace.com: The Basics

I'll begin by giving readers the basics on MySpace.com and Facebook.com.

MySpace.com is currently the top social networking site on the web. It boasts up to [110] million registered users, of whom 25% may be teenagers.

[In July 2005], Rupert Murdoch's News Corp. bought My Space for $580 million. Over the past year, traffic on MySpace has grown 318% ..., to 37.3 million visitors in February [2006].

MySpace says users must be at least 14. (The federal Children's Online Privacy Protection Act requires websites that target children under 13 to obtain "verifiable parental consent" before the kids can use the site; MySpace apparently didn't want to bother with the consent requirement.)

Free and ad-supported, MySpace allows users to post photos and music, and to stop by each other's sites to meet and mingle or hook up. Students can easily locate their classmates; MySpace maintains folders for various high schools and universities. Thus, MySpace can end up, in effect, hosting a virtual community that parallels a particular school or college—and often does.

But MySpace users need not belong to that community: If they so choose, they can customize their sites—blocking anyone but friends, for example. In addition, the site encourages users who feel they are being threatened by another member, to block that member and contact the police.

MySpace also reserves the right to terminate a user for engaging in threatening, lewd, or otherwise inappropriate behavior. And it will remove fake profiles by impersonators—a remedy that can be used by faculty, administrators or students who discover fake profiles claiming to be theirs.

In some instances, students engage in cyber-bullying—making critical remarks about other students or teachers.

Facebook.com: The Basics

Whereas MySpace.com is especially popular with teenagers, Facebook.com is especially popular with college students. Indeed, Facebook.com has claimed that it is used by 65% of undergrads at four-year colleges and universities. That amounts to more than 6.1 million students from more than 2,100 schools.

[In September 2005], Facebook expanded its reach to high-schoolers. At last count, a reported 900,000 had signed up. [As of April 2008, it has over 60 million members.]

Members can view full profiles of students from their own school. They can also search for other classmates by name, but if they locate them, they can see only the student's name, school and photo. To access a full profile, they must seek permission to be added to the student's list of "friends." Just as they can on MySpace.com, members also can impose further privacy limits—allowing access only to a chosen circle of friends.

Cases Where Postings Violate the Law

These sites—though a boon to students in many ways—have also raised their share of problems. And some of the problems may also involve torts, or violations of the criminal law.

In some instances, students engage in cyber-bullying—making critical remarks about other students or teachers. If these postings are factual, false, and damaging, they may count as defamation. The sites cannot be sued: Under a key provision of the Communications Decency Act, web intermediaries—those who merely allow others to post their own comments and photos—are not liable for defamation. But the authors can be.

Sometimes postings may be evidence of law-violation: In photos, underage subjects may be shown in sexually provocative poses, or shown smoking or drinking, or holding firearms. For instance, a 16-year-old boy in Jefferson, Colorado was arrested after police—having seen pictures on his My Space page in which he was holding handguns—found the weapons in his home. And in late April [2006], police reportedly intercepted a Columbine-style plot in Kansas on the basis of a threatening email posted on MySpace.com.

And sometimes postings may themselves violate the law—making criminal threats, or constituting harassment. In Costa

Mesa, California, twenty students were suspended from TeWinkle Middle School for two days for participating in a MySpace group where one student allegedly threatened to kill another and made anti-Semitic remarks.

Finally, sometimes postings can be an instrumentality of crime. Police have investigated allegations that teens were sexually assaulted by men they met on social networking sites. Indeed, the website Mycrimespace.com claims that various arrests of sexual predators are connected to users who have contacted their victims via MySpace.com

Do Students Have a First Amendment Defense?

Even if postings don't violate the law—or evidence or enable its violation—they may still break school rules, or evidence that these rules have been broken. For example, a gay student was recently expelled from a Christian university after the university found photos of him in drag on his MySpace.com page. The university said the student had violated its code of conduct, because his behavior was not consistent with Biblical values.

Moreover, even if rules are not broken, the postings may still trigger administrators to want to take punitive action such as suspension, expulsion, or putting a note on the student's record that may harm his or her chances of college admission, or on the job market.

Do students facing such actions have a First Amendment defense? Private high school students may be out of luck: their schools are not "government" actors, and the First Amendment does not apply.

(Also out of luck are students who are foolish enough to publicly criticize schools before they attend them: The Admissions Dean at Reed College in Portland, Oregon has noted that one application got rejected after disparaging Reed on the blogging site LiveJournal.com.)

In contrast, admitted students at public high schools, public colleges—and possibly private colleges that receive government money—may enjoy the First Amendment's protection for their online postings.

According to the U.S. Supreme Court, public school students don't "shed their constitutional right to freedom of speech or expression at the schoolhouse gate." Accordingly, in *Tinker v. Des Moines Independent Community School District*, the Court said public high school students had a First Amendment right to wear black armbands to class to protest the Vietnam War.

Student free-speech rights can be limited when the speech "materially disrupts classwork or involves substantial disorder or invasion of the rights of others"—and the armband-wearing, the Court said in *Tinker*, didn't meet the test.

What kind of limitations have been upheld?

In *Bethel School District No. 403 v. Fraser*, the Court ruled that a high school student whose student-government-nomination speech included "obscene, profane language or gestures" could constitutionally be suspended.

And in *Hazelwood Sch. Dist. v. Kuhlmeier*, the Court okayed censorship of a school-sponsored newspaper that was "reasonably related to legitimate pedagogical concerns."

But the *Hazelwood* ruling was limited in important ways. It applied only to censorship of "school-sponsored publications, theatrical productions, and other expressive activities that students, parents, and members of the public might reasonably perceive to bear the imprimatur of the school"—and it did not apply to even school-sponsored publications that had been opened as "public forums for student expression." (Finally, it's clear the standard would not apply to college newspapers.)

First Amendment Arguments Won— and Lost

Let's look at a few specific cases.

In 2000, a federal court in the Western District of Washington State held—in *Emmett v. Kent School District*—that public school officials could not punish a student Nick Emmett for postings on a website, referred to as the "Unofficial Kentlake High Home Page." Emmett and his friends—after being given the task of penning their own obituaries, in a creative writing class—had run afoul of school officials by posting a parody obituary for another classmate.

When [social networking or blogging] originates off campus, a student has a First Amendment right to make even unpleasant, critical remarks.

The court pointed out that at no time were school funds [or computers] involved with the website. Accordingly, the court held that "[a]lthough the intended audience was undoubtedly connected to Kentlake High School, the speech was entirely outside of the school's supervision or control."

Most courts to address such cases have agreed: When the publication originates off campus, a student has a First Amendment right to make even unpleasant, critical remarks.

Occasionally, however, courts have applied *Tinker*'s "material disruption" standard even to off-campus speech.

For example, in 1998, in *Beussink v. Woodland School District*, a federal court in the Eastern District of Missouri inquired whether a public high school student's site using vulgar language to criticize his school and its faculty fulfilled *Tinker*'s standard. (As in the *Emmett* case, the site was created outside of the classroom, with the student's own computer and Internet connection; the court noted, however, that a classmate had viewed the site at school.) The court ultimately held that the site was First Amendment-protected because it was not materially disruptive.

Likewise, in 2002, in *J.S. ex rel H.S. v. Bethlehem Area School District*, the Supreme Court of Pennsylvania applied

Tinker even though a website was not created at school, on the ground that the site "was aimed at a specific school and/or its personnel" and was "brought onto the school campus or accessed at school by its originator."

And there—unlike in the Missouri case—the court found a "material disruption" occurred: The site included an image in which a teacher's decapitated head dripped with blood and a request that visitors contribute $20 for a hit man. The site also showed an image of the same teacher's face transforming into Hitler's.

The "hit man" request came perilously close to a criminal threat or solicitation—a fact of which the court no doubt took notice. As noted above, when it comes to First Amendment protection here, we're talking about speech that isn't criminal: If a student publishes a physical threat toward another student, or a teacher or administrator, the Constitution won't protect that.

Criticism, though, is fair play. Just this month [in May 2006], New Jersey's Oceanport School District this month paid a $117,500 settlement to 17-year-old Ryan Dwyer after a district court ruled that [the district] had violated his First Amendment rights by punishing him for a website blasting his middle school and some faculty members.

Mr. Dwyer wrote, among other things, "MAPLE PLACE IS THE WORST SCHOOL ON THE PLANET!" and "The Principal, Dr. Amato, is not your friend and is a dictator."

These messages—classic statements of opinion—weren't defamatory. They received full First Amendment protection.

How Can Students Learn the Rules?

The Electronic Frontier Foundation (EFF), a San Francisco-based digital-rights advocacy group, recently released a legal guide for student bloggers, which provides practical guidance by addressing questions such as,

"So can I criticize teachers on my blog?"

The EFF is critical of the courts that have applied *Tinker*'s "material disruption" standard to privately-written student blogs and web pages. But it rightly warns students that this standard could be applied—especially if their comments are very outrageous and offensive in the way they target teacher or peers. The EFF guide also advises students to cool off before posting hateful comments or very sensitive private details about themselves and their classmates.

Meanwhile, those students, teachers, and administrators who feel they've been made the target of MySpace posting should remember that while they may not always have a legal remedy, they may have a practical one: They can ask the site to de-post the offensive material—and if it does, users can't invoke the First Amendment when they complain.

As a private entity, MySpace isn't obligated to honor users' First Amendment rights. And under that Communications Decency Act (CDA) provision, it can completely feel free to remove postings at its discretion: The very reason the CDA allows sites to operate liability-free, is to make sure they can police their sites for postings they find harmful or offensive, without fear of incurring liability as a result of doing so.

13

Educational Software Can Increase Learning

Judi Mathis Johnson

Judi Mathis Johnson is a faculty member for the technology in education division at Lesley University, which has campus locations in the United States and Israel.

Throughout the past three decades, the development of educational software has been marked both by trial-and-error and moderate success. From its lofty beginnings in research facilities of the 1960s to current-day personal digital assistants (PDAs) and the global positioning system (GPS), researchers, educators, and students are embarking on the further development of educational software that will greatly benefit learning in the future. Educational software is not yet perfect and is experiencing an awkward "adolescent" phase, as evidenced by its long history in the classroom and computer lab. But its potential as a multimedia learning application has wide appeal to students of many strengths and weaknesses and many important advantages over books and other conventional classroom tools.

Software translates the computer's possibilities into results. Innovative software provides new and sometimes unexpected results. Educational software has the added responsibility of stimulating student cognitive growth that can be measured using traditional and performance-based assessment. The most difficult software to create and the most rewarding is a combination of the two—innovative educational software.

Judi Mathis Johnson, "Then, Now, and Beyond . . . A Look at the Past 30 Years of Educational Software," *Learning and Leading with Technology*, vol. 30, April 2003, pp. 6–13.

Federal and state governing agents are now requiring measurable education results before allocating further funds for technology. In the 2001 No Child Left Behind legislation in the United States, software companies have been informed that if schools use federal monies to purchase their products, then the companies must provide research results that demonstrate their products' effectiveness. For some educational software companies, research has been a natural part of their process. Supporting research is only new to those companies unfamiliar with the history of educational software. Many lessons can be gleaned from the past development of educational software to help guide future development. I highlight 15 of these lessons as they come up in this article. . . .

Once software has been created from a research base, then the dissemination and integration begin. . . .

The history of commercial software can be traced through the development of games, which parallels the development of hardware. The faster and more powerful the hardware is, the more visually complex the commercial software is. Educational software creation has not been as sensitive to hardware and economic trends; development has been more closely linked to educators, their research, dissemination, and creative genius.

Lofty Beginnings

Provide educators with mainframe computers and wonderful, creative things can happen. Early software projects were firmly embedded in a research environment. During the 1960s, The University of Utah, Stanford University, The University of Illinois, and Massachusetts Institute of Technology (MIT) were incubators for creating a solid foundation in the early creation of educational software. Developers created software based on educational research results and constantly worked with students and classroom teachers to test results as they developed curriculum.

These four groups created more than just a body of instructional software: they established the importance of proving the effectiveness of any software before making it available for purchase (Lesson 1). In some cases, their product names are synonymous with their company names: WICAT (World Institute for Computer-Assisted Teaching), CCC (Computer Curriculum Corporation), PLATO (Programmed Logic for Automated Teaching Outcomes), and Logo.

Two large projects combined instruction and assessment. Drill and practice was at the core of WICAT's materials and demonstrated the effectiveness of their mission. CCC's Patrick Suppes had a wealth of riches, including a mainframe computer and eager graduate students in education, to study how to design high-quality mathematics instruction materials. Suppes's work formed the foundation of his company. Both projects demonstrated that assessment and instructional software could be combined effectively (Lesson 2). The computer can provide instruction, assess student work, and manage assessment results. At CCC, the software delivered instruction using extremely well-designed questions and assessed students' answers to determine which problems to pose next. This early expert system is modeled on a one-on-one tutoring session with a student, where the tutor provides practice for poorly understood concepts and advances the student after he or she has successfully completed problems.

PLATO stamped its name on a body of software. However, its effects may be greater as a project that spawned a community that incubated many of the early ideas later incorporated into Internet programs. Connected to the computers were faculty members, graduate students, local teachers, and classroom students. TUTOR was the authoring language they created to enable everyone to create simple or complex programs, post on the mainframe, and share with others. By 1987, PLATO provided more than 12,000 hours of instruction in more than 100 subjects with a wide range of quality and pedagogical approaches. A connected education community models how to improve education and software simultaneously (Lesson 3).

PLATO's simple Notes system for communicating about program problems provided the basis for its later e-mail system. Simple software tools need to be available for teachers to communicate classroom results (Lesson 4).

MIT was the home for Seymour Papert, his powerful ideas, and a turtle that responded to commands in Logo. The programming language Logo was first available on a mainframe, and initial microcomputer versions were available for the Apple, Atari, and Texas Instruments (TI) computers. How children think and learn was at the heart of this development. With powerful tools in hand, students can produce powerful ideas (Lesson 5).

Using Logo effectively required staff development and a greater understanding of learning theory than just a course on human development. Math teachers could immediately see the amount of mathematics in Logo, but might not be accustomed to teaching using the discovery method. Most English teachers were never exposed to the List processes built into Logo that could enhance language development. Logo embodies a pedagogy—discovery. If the teacher does not teach using this instructional approach, the students' experiences may not be as full as originally imagined. Dissemination should include staff development as well as software availability (Lesson 6).

Success for the three mainframe projects was based on assessment of traditionally tested curriculum. However, success of a student using Logo was more challenging to evaluate. Often time on task and student interest is foremost in the assessment report. Long-term testing is still needed to see whether students think in different ways, use different parts of their brains, or have had different levels of success in adulthood.

Much of this software from these four groups is still available today in some form or another. The CCC and PLATO software now co-reside under the roof of Pearson Education and provide content For NovaNet. Logo Computer Systems, Inc., in Canada, continues to produce problem-solving software that embodies programmable microworlds for developing problem-solving skills. LEGO Mindstorms is a present-day commercial robotic kit that carries on the love of programming and creating knowledge.

Golden Age of Creative Stand-alone Software

The invention of the microcomputer, the proliferation of Radio Shack businesses on every corner, and the growing number of teachers who had worked with mainframes and instruction combined to spark the emergence of simple stand-alone, programs. Nearly all of the microcomputers from the late 1970s and early 1980s came with some version of the BASIC programming language. BASIC became a course to be taught and an environment for creating student programs.

Authoring languages were once prevalent. Preservice teachers used Apple Pilot to create interactive programs and develop a deeper understanding about teaching and learning. Other authoring opportunities included BLOCKS (an authoring language developed by the Kyde Tyme Project led by Ted Perry from the San Juan Unified School District and the Project at Berkeley, California's School for the Deaf), dBase for handling data, and HyperCard (based on HyperTalk, the scripting language) for creating multidirectional connectivity.

Each program was only as good as the original programmer, who was probably a hobbyist, not a professional. Unfortunately, a program written for one microcomputer usually wouldn't run on another. A quick list of microcomputers, each with their own version of BASIC, found in schools must include a Commodore Pet (and later the 64), an Atari XL/XE,

Radio Shack Level I or II or the later TRS-80, Apple II (II+, IIc, IIe, and IIGS), TI and later the IBM jr. and the Sinclair. Obviously, distributing this software to other educators was a major challenge. When teachers tried to share their programs, it became evident that sharing the directions for how to use the program in the classroom could be critical to its success.

MECC [Minnesota Educational Computing Consortium] led the way toward a solution, modeling how companies could distribute a large collection of software first on mainframe and later on diskettes and CD-ROMs. In the 1980s and early 1990s, a MECC license allowed schools to copy and create disks from masters. MECC consistently provided classroom documentation to support their programs. High-quality support material can be critical to software's success in the classroom (Lesson 7).

Between 1978 and 1983, some of the most creative programs for students were produced. Educators began to look beyond the replication of existing educational practices to procedure programs that were colorful, simple to use, engaging, challenging, and embraced student learning. Snooper Troops, Gertrude's Puzzles, Teasers by Tobbs, The Factory, Rocky's Boots, and Muppets on Parade were just a few of the stimulating and innovative titles. Most titles dealt with problem solving and made the basic assumption students could develop thinking skills *and* have an enjoyable experience (Lesson 8).

Teachers saw the potential of the technology to engage student thinking and authored many excellent titles during this period. They also illuminated the way to rethink what students need to be taught when technology is regularly available. Always rethink the curriculum and methodologies when using any software with students (Lesson 9).

Early programs also modeled excellent learning environments. Marge (Cappo) Kosel, a teacher in Minnesota, developed Odell Lake and the simply named K-2 diskette. The K-2 diskette was one of the very few at that time that used single keystrokes for students to answer questions—a critical feature for young computer-using children that is now common.

Success of software in the classroom was often based on student engagement criteria, such as time on task and enjoyment ratings. However, enjoyment is only one measure of a software program's success. Rarely were students tested on the content being taught. This lack of integration into the classroom assessment helped keep computer use in the classroom to a marginal level and not widely integrated.

Opportunities for Authentic Learning

The next major change in the development of educational software was the maturation of educational tools. The first tools were simple and too often viewed as teacher, not student, tools. Some examples were Crossword Magic, Tic Tac Show, Game Show, and numerous spelling programs. Teachers entered their own content for students, but the task could be too time-consuming to be regularly integrated.

These first software tools allowed teachers to tailor the content. This allows assessment to be focused on specific local and state standards (Lesson 10). However, control over the curriculum content of software has almost become removed from the teacher in most new software titles.

The tools that have matured and gained success in the classroom are tools that provide authentic experiences. Students write using a word processor, draft using CAD programs, create and test original geometry theories using a geometry constructor, and conduct research using database managers that professionals use (Lesson 11). This set of tools provided new ways for students to learn, express their knowledge, and extend their thinking. These tools also challenged how we measure success, what we teach, what we assess, and how we assess student learning.

Some exemplary authentic tools that have emerged over the past decade are Kid Pix, HyperStudio, TimeLiner, Inspiration, and Geometer's Sketchpad. The power of each tool is greater than just what students are capable of doing using it. Teachers use these programs to teach differently than before. Curriculum is changed to incorporate these tools and because of what these tools enable students to do.

However, technology tools need to be taught with instructional material from within a content area (Lesson 12). For example, Visicalc was a great spreadsheet, but Cruncher is a tool for teaching mathematics that uses a spreadsheet. The sophistication of a tool is not as important in the classroom as its ability to help students begin to think differently because they have those tools available.

External Influences

Educational software has been influenced by hardware developments (though not as dramatically as commercial software has) and commercial software companies.

Hardware Variety. Hardware seems to change almost daily. Educators need to be aware of new opportunities and think about what their students need to learn. But teachers do not need to bring in every new piece of technology just because it is new. Teachers need to select hardware to test with students based on how the technology empowers students (Lesson 13).

The discussion of educational software should never be limited to one medium, such as a CD-ROM—just as hardware should never be limited to just desktop computers. Laser videodiscs allowed teachers to use extensive video effectively years before the CD-ROM became the standard. Handheld computers have grown from the four-function calculator to graphing calculators with interactive programs. The global positioning system (GPS) has stimulated some thought about the future of its use in the classroom; this tool is rapidly being integrated in most other personal tools. The personal digital assistant

(PDA or handheld) is currently being tested to see how best to both use it in the classroom and extend the classroom to other locales. These technologies demand new types of software and new methods of distribution such as wireless and the Internet.

Text-only encyclopedias were biased toward the linguistically strong student. Multimedia encyclopedias . . . stimulate a wider range of students.

Commercial Influence. The power of software companies cannot be taken lightly. Under the classification of edutainment software, companies tried to convince the public that many commercial titles contained educational or content value. Edutainment may captivate and sometimes titillate, but rarely can it satiate. Fortunately, their 15 minutes has passed, and educators can focus on more important values, such as student learning.

Although some software may have been produced using federal funding (e.g., NSF [National Science Foundation] grants) or by public universities, often the distribution is dependent on commercial companies. Although willing to handle products for distribution, companies rarely provide for more than three years of product support. Typically, educators learn about a product during its first year. During the second year, software may be tested in some schools willing to take risks to examine its potential. Only in the third year will real integration begin to bring about some curricular changes and broader classroom effectiveness. Unfortunately, at this point, the software may no longer be available for purchase. Educational products require years of support (Lesson 14). Some of the programs no longer available include the whole set of Microsoft Home products, which included 500 Nations and the History of Musical Instruments; Rocky's Boots, which was never made for anything other than the early PCs; and Freedom Trail, which was an excellent program about the Underground Railroad.

Some Success Stories

Some software titles have made significant changes in our schools. For example, encyclopedias will never be text-only again. Students' learning styles vary. Text-only encyclopedias were biased toward the linguistically strong student. Multimedia encyclopedias have movement, color, sound, and a variety of organizational structures (other than alphabetical order) that stimulate a wider range of students.

Geometry instruction has also changed because of the introduction of software. Before software use was common, students could explore geometric ideas on paper, but not to the extent or with the ease they can using such software as Geometric Explorers (from the early days) and Geometer's Sketchpad (a current product). From the beginning, students explored geometry as mathematicians, trying and testing ideas. An unexpected but highly desirable result has been the production of original geometry theorems posed and proven by high school students using these tools. Powerful tools in the hands of learners can produce original thought (Lessons 15).

Educational software development is still in that awkward adolescent stage where guidance is still needed, variations of quality are to be expected, but greatness can be possible.

Accountability

The list of educational software titles over the past few decades is full of titles that are no longer available. Some were well designed and could still be of value, such as 500 Nations. But the majority were attempts to do the same thing without rethinking the learning environment of the computer, such as the many storybooks that had no interactivity or glossary.

The past also includes exemplars to study and identify how to create more programs in the future. A key element missing from too many current educational programs is the ability for the teacher to modify the content to meet class or individual needs or curriculum guidelines.

But the future should hold many collaborative efforts. Universities (research centers), classroom teachers, and companies can work together to create programs that are educationally sound, classroom friendly, have support materials to assist dissemination, engage the learner, and meet standards. If software programs' code were open source, then any teacher could share his or her modifications with any other teacher. Meeting state-mandated goals could be easily embedded into programs within a few years through a state-sponsored sharing site.

The exciting infant years are past, where everything was new and refreshing even if it wasn't useful. Many false steps have been taken, and not all that is good has been retained. Educational software development is still in that awkward adolescent stage where guidance is still needed, variations of quality are to be expected, but greatness can be possible.

14

Educational Software May Not Increase Learning

U.S. Department of Education

Established in 1980, the U.S. Department of Education (ED) aims to promote student achievement, establish policies on federal financial aid for education, focus national attention on key educational issues, and prohibit discrimination, ensuring equal access to education.

The increasing use of educational software in U.S. schools comes at mounting costs. Therefore, concerns about the added academic benefits, or lack thereof, of such technology deserve credence. A recent one-year study of grade school students who used selected educational software in class shows it may not significantly raise reading and mathematics scores. In addition, in classes where educational software was used, students were less likely to participate in class and more likely to be working independently. This study, however, does not investigate the effectiveness of educational software in aiding students with disabilities or teaching skills that depend on technology. And a second-year study will be conducted with the same teachers and students in case more experience using educational software indeed results in additional academic improvement.

With computers now commonplace in American classrooms, and districts facing substantial costs of hardware and software, concerns naturally arise about the contri-

U.S. Department of Education, "Effectiveness of Reading and Mathematics Software Products: Findings from the First Student Cohort: Executive Summary," March 2007, pp. xii–xvi, xviii, xviv.

bution of this technology to students' learning. The No Child Left Behind Act (P.L. 107-110, section 2421) called for the U.S. Department of Education (ED) to conduct a national study of the effectiveness of educational technology. This legislation also called for the study to use "scientifically based research methods and control groups or control conditions" and to focus on the impact of technology on student academic achievement.

Test scores were not significantly higher in classrooms using selected reading and mathematics software products.

In 2003, ED contracted with Mathematica Policy Research, Inc. (MPR) and SRI International to conduct the study. The team worked with ED to select technology products; recruit school districts, schools, and teachers; test students; observe classrooms; and analyze the data. The study used an experimental design to assess the effects of technology products, with volunteering teachers randomly assigned to use or not use selected products.

The main findings of the study are:

1. *Test Scores Were Not Significantly Higher in Classrooms Using Selected Reading and Mathematics Software Products.* Test scores in treatment classrooms that were randomly assigned to use products did not differ from test scores in control classrooms by statistically significant margins.

2. *Effects Were Correlated With Some Classroom and School Characteristics.* For reading products, effects on overall test scores were correlated with the student-teacher ratio in first grade classrooms and with the amount of time that products were used in fourth grade classrooms. For math products, effects were uncorrelated with classroom and school characteristics.

Educational technology is used for word processing, presentation, spreadsheets, databases, internet search, distance education, virtual schools, interactions with simulations and models, and collaboration over local and global networks. Technology also is used as assistive devices for students with disabilities and to teach concepts or skills that are difficult or impossible to convey without technology. This study is specifically focused on whether students had higher reading or math test scores when teachers had access to selected software products designed to support learning in reading or mathematics. It was not designed to assess the effectiveness of educational technology across its entire spectrum of uses, and the study's findings do not support conclusions about technology's effectiveness beyond the study's context, such as in other subject areas.

This report is the first of two from the study. Whether reading and mathematics software is more effective when teachers have more experience using it is being examined with a second year of data. The second year involves teachers who were in the first data collection (those who are teaching in the same school and at the same grade level or subject area) and a second cohort of students. The second report will present effects for individual products. The current report will present effects for groups of products.

Selecting Technology Products for the Study

The study was based on the voluntary participation of technology product developers, districts and schools, and teachers. Their characteristics provide an important part of the study's structure and context for interpreting its findings.

Before products could be selected, decisions were needed about the study's focus. The legislation mandating the study provided general guidelines but did not describe specifically how the study was to be implemented. A design team consisting of U.S. Department of Education staff, researchers from

MPR and its partners, and researchers and educational technology experts recommended that the study

- focus attention on technology products that support reading or math instruction in low-income schools serving the K-12 grades;

- use an experimental design to ensure that measured achievement gains could be attributed to products; and

- base the analysis of student academic achievement on a commonly used standardized test.

The team also identified conditions and practices whose relationships to effectiveness could be studied, and recommended a public process in which developers of technology products would be invited to provide information that a panel would consider in its selection of products for the study. A design report provided discussion and rationales for the recommendations. . . .

The voluntary aspect of company participation in the study meant that products were not a representative sampling of reading and math technology used in schools. Not all products were submitted for consideration by the study, and most products that were submitted were not selected. Also, products that were selected were able to provide at least some evidence of effectiveness from previous research. ED recognized that selecting ostensibly more effective products could tilt the study toward finding higher levels of effectiveness, but the tilt was viewed as a reasonable tradeoff to avoid investing the study's resources in products that had little or no evidence of effectiveness.

The study was designed to report results for groups of products rather than for individual products. Congress asked whether technology was effective and not how the effectiveness of individual products compared. Further, a study designed to determine the effectiveness of groups of products required fewer classrooms and schools to achieve a target level of statistical precision and thus had lower costs than a study designed to determine the effectiveness of individual products at the same level of precision. Developers of software products volunteered to participate in the study with the understanding that the results would be reported only for groups of products.

During the course of implementing the study, various parties expressed an interest in knowing results for individual products. To accommodate that interest, the design of the study was modified in its second year of data collection. At the same time, product developers were asked to consent to having individual results about their products reported in the second year of data collection. A report of the results from the second year is forthcoming.

Recruiting Districts and Schools for the Study

After products were selected, the study team began recruiting school districts to participate. The team focused on school districts that had low student achievement and large proportions of students in poverty, but these were general guidelines rather than strict eligibility criteria. The study sought districts and schools that did not already use products like those in the study so that there would be a contrast between the use of technology in treatment and control classrooms. Product vendors suggested many of the districts that ultimately participated in the study. Others had previously participated in studies with MPR or learned of the study from news articles and contacted MPR to express interest.

Interested districts identified schools for the study that fell within the guidelines. Generally, schools were identified by senior district staff based on broad considerations, such as whether schools had adequate technology infrastructure and whether schools were participating in other initiatives. By September 2004, the study had recruited 33 districts and 132 schools to participate. Five districts elected to implement products in two or more grade levels, and one district decided to implement a product in all four grade levels, resulting in 45 combinations of districts and product implementations. Districts and schools in the study had higher-than-average poverty levels and minority student populations.

To implement the experimental design, the study team randomly assigned volunteering teachers in participating schools to use products (the "treatment group") or not (the "control group"). Because of the experimental design, teachers in the treatment and control groups were expected to be equivalent, on average, except that one group is using one of the study's technology products. Aspects of teaching that are difficult or impossible to observe, such as a teacher's ability to motivate students to learn, are "controlled" by the experimental design because teachers were randomly assigned, and therefore should be the same in both groups, on average. The study also used statistical methods to adjust for remaining differences in measured characteristics of schools, teachers, and students, which arise because of sampling variability. . . .

At the end of trainings, most teachers reported that they were prepared to use the products with their classes.

Summary of Study Findings

The four grade levels essentially comprise substudies within the overall study, and findings are reported separately for each. The study's data collection approach was the same for the four substudies.

The implementation analysis focused on how products were used in classrooms, their extent of usage, issues that resulted from their use, and how their use affected classroom activities. Three implementation findings emerged consistently across the four substudies:

1. *Nearly All Teachers Received Training and Believed the Training Prepared Them to Use the Products.* Vendors trained teachers in summer and early fall of 2004 on using products. Nearly all teachers attended trainings (94 percent to 98 percent, depending on the grade level). At the end of trainings, most teachers reported that they were confident that they were prepared to use the products with their classes. Generally, teachers reported a lower degree of confidence in what they had learned after they began using products in the classroom.

2. *Technical Difficulties Using Products Mostly Were Minor.* Minor technical difficulties in using products, such as issues with students logging in, computers locking up, or hardware problems such as headphones not working, were fairly common. Most of the technical difficulties were easily corrected or worked around. When asked whether they would use the products again, nearly all teachers indicated that they would.

On average, after one year, products did not increase or decrease test scores by amounts that were statistically different from zero.

---

3. *When Products Were Being Used, Students Were More Likely to Engage in Individual Practice and Teachers Were More Likely to Facilitate Student Learning Rather Than Lecture.* Data from classroom observations indicated that, compared to students in control classrooms where the same subject was taught without using the selected products, students using products were more likely to be observed working with academic content on their own and less likely to be listening to a lecture or participating in question-and-answer sessions. Treatment teachers were more likely than control teachers to be observed

working with individual students to facilitate their learning (such as by pointing out key ideas or giving hints or suggestions on tackling the task students were working on) rather than leading whole-class activities.

Comparing student test scores for treatment teachers using study products and control teachers not using study products is the study's measure of product effectiveness. Effects on test scores were estimated using a statistical model that accounts for correlations of students within classrooms and classrooms within schools. The robustness of the results was assessed by examining findings using different methods of estimation and using district test scores as outcomes, and the patterns of findings were similar. . . .

Congress posed questions about the effectiveness of educational technology and how effectiveness is related to conditions and practices. The study identified reading and mathematics software products based on prior evidence of effectiveness and other criteria and recruited districts, schools, and teachers to implement the products. On average, after one year, products did not increase or decrease test scores by amounts that were statistically different from zero.

For first and fourth grade reading products, the study found several school and classroom characteristics that were correlated with effectiveness, including student-teacher ratios (for first grade) and the amount of time products were used (for fourth grade). The study did not find characteristics related to effectiveness for sixth grade math or algebra. The study also found that products caused teachers to be less likely to lecture and more likely to facilitate, while students using reading or mathematics software products were more likely to be working on their own.

The results reported here are based on schools and teachers who were not using the products in the previous school year. Whether products are more effective when teachers have more experience using them is being examined with a second year of data. The study will involve teachers who were in the first data collection (those who are teaching in the same school and at the same grade level or subject area) and a new group of students. The second-year study will also report results separately for the various products.

Organizations to Contact

The editors have compiled the following list of organizations concerned with the issues debated in this book. The descriptions are derived from materials provided by the organizations. All have publications or information available for interested readers. The list was compiled on the date of publication of the present volume; the information provided here may change. Be aware that many organizations take several weeks or longer to respond to inquiries, so allow as much time as possible.

American Federation of Teachers (AFT)
555 New Jersey Avenue, NW, Washington, DC   20001
(202) 879-4400
Web site: www.aft.org

The AFT was founded in 1916 to represent the economic, social and professional interests of classroom teachers. It has more than 3,000 local affiliates nationwide, 43 state affiliates, and more than 1.3 million members. It publishes the *PSRP Reporter*, a quarterly newsletter.

The Carnegie Foundation for the Advancement of Teaching
51 Vista Lane, Stanford, CA   94305
(650) 566-5100 • fax: (650) 326-0278
Web site: www.carnegiefoundation.org

Established in 1905, the Carnegie Foundation is an independent policy and research center that specializes in teaching. Its program areas include K-12, undergraduate, graduate, and professional education. It produces many publications, including the higher education–centered *Change* magazine.

DO-IT (Disabilities, Opportunities, Internetworking and Technology)
Box 355670, Seattle, WA   98195-5670

e-mail: doit@u.washington.edu
Web site: www.washington.edu/doit

DO-IT is a project based at the University of Washington, Seattle, that helps individuals with disabilities transition to college and careers. It promotes the use of computer and networking technologies to increase independence, productivity, and participation in education and employment. DO-IT offers training materials, videos, and publications including the newsletter *DO-IT News.*

International Society for Technology in Education (ISTE)
1710 Rhode Island Avenue, NW, Washington, DC   20036
(800) 336-5191 • fax (541) 302-3778
e-mail: iste@iste.org
Web site: www.iste.org

A nonprofit membership organization, ISTE provides leadership and service to improve teaching, learning, and school leadership by advancing the effective use of technology in PK-12 and teacher education. Home of the National Educational Technology Standards (NETS), the Center for Applied Research in Educational Technology (CARET), and the National Educational Computing Conference (NECC), ISTE represents more than 85,000 professionals worldwide.

Internet Society (ISOC)
1775 Wiehle Avenue, Reston, VA   20190-5108
(703) 326-9880 • fax: (703) 326-9881
e-mail isoc@isoc.org
Web site: www.isoc.org

A group of technologists, developers, educators, researchers, government representatives, and businesspeople, ISOC supports the development and dissemination of standards for the Internet and works to ensure global cooperation and coordination for the Internet and related Internet-working technologies and applications. It produces a variety of publications, including the bimonthly magazine *On the Internet.*

National Education Association (NEA)
1201 16th Street, NW, Washington, DC   20036-3290
(202) 833-4000 • (202) 822-7974
Web site: www.nea.org

NEA is a volunteer-based organization that represents 3.2 million public school teachers, university and college faculty members, college students training to be teachers, retired educators, and other educational professionals. It has affiliate organizations in every state and publishes the electronic newsletter *NEA Today*.

U.S. Department of Education (ED)
400 Maryland Avenue, SW, Washington, D.C.   20202
(800) USA-LEARN (872-5327)
Web site: www.ed.gov

Established in 1980, ED aims to promote student achievement, establish policies on federal financial aid for education, focus national attention on key educational issues, and prohibit discrimination, ensuring equal access to education. The Web site offers several different publications such as press releases, speeches, fact sheets, newsletters, and journals.

Bibliography

Books

Tara Brabazon   *Digital Hemlock: Internet Education and the Poisoning of Teaching.* Sydney, AU: University of New South Wales Press, 2003.

Clayton M. Christensen, Curtis W. Johnson, and Michael B. Horn   *Disrupting Class: How Disruptive Innovation Will Change the Way the World Learns.* New York: McGraw-Hill, 2008.

Williams Clyde and Andrew Delohery   *Using Technology in Education.* New Haven, CT: Yale University Press, 2005.

Claudia Goldin and Lawrence F. Katz   *The Race Between Education and Technology.* Cambridge, MA: Belknap Press, 2008.

James Paul Gee   *What Video Games Have to Teach Us About Learning and Literacy,* 2nd edition. New York: Palgrave Macmillan, 2007.

Mary E. Hess   *Engaging Technology in Theological Education: All That We Can't Leave Behind.* Lanham, MD: Rowman & Littlefield Publishers, 2005.

David Hutchison   *Playing to Learn: Video Games in the Classroom.* Westport, CT: Teacher Ideas Press, 2007.

Joe Lockard and Mark Pegrum, eds.
Brave New Classrooms: Democratic Education and the Internet. New York: Peter Lang Publishing, 2006.

Marc Prensky
Don't Bother Me Mom—I'm Learning. St. Paul, MN: Paragon House Publishers, 2006.

Olivia N. Saracho and Bernard Spodek, eds.
Contemporary Perspectives on Science and Technology in Early Childhood Education. Charlotte, NC: Information Age Publishing, 2007.

Harold Wenglinksy
Using Technology Wisely: The Keys To Success In Schools. New York: Teachers College Press, 2005.

Periodicals

Kate Baggott
"Literacy and Text Messaging: How Will the Next Generation Read and Write?" *Technology Review*, December 21, 2006.

Brenda J. Buote
"Home Schooled," *Boston Globe*, May 15, 2008.

John Cox
"Higher Education Struggles to Recast Classrooms with Technology; Online Learning Techniques, Strategies Change Face of Education," *Network World*, March 21, 2007.

eSchool News
"Blogging Helps Encourage Teen Writing," *eSchool News*, April 30, 2008.

Ben Feller   "Scientists: Video Games Can Reshape Education," *USA Today*, October 18, 2006.

James Paul Gee   "High Score Education," *Wired*, May 2003.

Patrick Greene   "The Potential of Gaming on K-12 Education," *Multimedia & Internet@Schools*, May–June 2006.

Ann McClure   "Distant, Not Absent: Keeping Online Learners Engaged Can Help Them Reach the Finish Line," *University Business*, November 2007.

Kirsten Nelson   "Hardly a Blank Slate—Electronic Whiteboard Technology Enhances Classroom Learning," *Government Video*, May 1, 2006.

Amit R. Paley   "Software's Benefits on Tests in Doubt," *Washington Post*, April 5, 2007.

Will Richardson   "What's a Wiki? A Powerful Collaboration Tool for Learning. That's What!" *Multimedia & Internet@Schools*, November–December 2005.

Rodney P. Riegle   "Viewpoint: Online Courses as Video Games," *Campus Technology*, June 14, 2005.

Terrie Hale
Scheckelhoff

"Girls & Technology: How Can We Support Girls in Integrating Technologies More Fully in Their Learning," *Library Media Connection*, August–September 2006.

Del Siegle

"Podcasts and Blogs: Learning Opportunities on the Information Highway," *Gifted Child Today*, Summer 2007.

David Warlick

"A Day in the Life of Web 2.0: The Latest Powerful Online Tools Can Be Harnessed to Transform and Expand the Learning Experience," *Technology & Learning*, October 2006.

Index